# New England's
# Legacy
# of
# Shipwrecks

By
## Henry Keatts

**AMERICAN MERCHANT MARINE MUSEUM PRESS**
United States Merchant Marine Academy
Kings Point, New York

International Standard Book Number 0-936849-02-9


Published by
American Merchant Marine Museum Press
United States Merchant Marine Academy
Kings Point, New York


Distributed by
Fathom Press
P.O. Box 191
Eastport, New York 11941

Front cover photograph of the *Bass* by Brad Sheard
Back cover photograph by Steve Bielenda

## Dedication

To my wife Carole, a beautiful woman and an excellent diver.

## Publisher's Note

The American Merchant Marine Museum Press will publish a second volume, authored by Professor Keatts, on New England shipwrecks. If you have information or suggestions you would like to share, please mail them directly to Professor Henry Keatts, Suffolk County Community College, Riverhead, New York 11901. Also, any surface or underwater photographs you would like to have considered for publication should be sent directly to Professor Keatts. Those supplying information will be acknowledged and photographers will be credited for their contributions.

In addition, Professor Keatts is working on Volume I of New York and New Jersey shipwrecks. He would appreciate any information or photographs of sunken ships in that area.

## Acknowledgements

Without the contributions and cooperation of the following individuals and organizations, this book would not have been possible:

Frank Benoit
Fred Benson
Steve Bielenda
Ralph Blood
Richard Boonisar
Bill Campbell
Gary Carbonneau
Bill Carter
Bob Cartier
Mike Casalino
Dave Clancy
Chip Cooper

David Cox
Michael deCamp
Jim Dolph
George Farr
Steve Gato
Paul Goudreau
Aaron Hirsch
Chris Hugo
Jon Hulburt
Scott Jenkins
Bill Kurz
Jerry Lawrence

Brad Luther
Jeff Miller
Paul Morris
Bill Palmer
Bill Quinn
Tom Roach
Gardner Roberts
Brad Sheard
Paul Sherman
Brian Skerry

The Mariners' Museum
The Peabody Museum of Salem
Steamship Historical Society
Univ. of Baltimore Library
U.S. Naval Institute
Historical Maritime Group of New England
Block Island Historical Society
Naval Historical Center
Portland Press Herald
National Archives
Portsmouth Naval Shipyard
Library of Congress
U.S. Coast Guard
The Brick Store Museum
EG & G

Thanks to George J. Hiltner III of Reader Friendly Enterprises for proof-reading and copy-editing.

# Preface

The remains of wrecked ships abound along the rugged New England Coast. Indeed, in the minds of many, the two are almost synonymous— with little wonder. Several thousand vessels have sunk along that shore since colonial times—victims of winter storms, dense fog, military conflict, human error, inhospitable shores.

The shipwrecks in this book are popular dive spots visited by many sport divers each year. However, few of those who dive know the particulars of the wreck they are visiting. They may know little more than the name of the ship and the approximate year it sank. Familiarity with its history adds a new dimension of interest to the exploration of a shipwreck. When and why was the vessel built? How was she used? What did she accomplish? Why was she at the site of her sinking? What were the sea conditions? What steps were taken to avoid the disaster? Was rescue attempted? Were there survivors? Was salvage attempted? With answers to such questions, divers are no longer just examining spars, ribs, sheathing and fittings. They are exploring an historic relic where men lived and laughed, ate and drank, fought and played, and the history provides a context for exploration.

The purpose of this volume is to provide the history of each vessel and describe its present condition. For more than a decade, I have gathered as much information on shipwrecks as possible. That research has revealed that the Northeast Coast of the United States is one of the best scuba diving areas in the world, at least for the number, variety and fascination of its shipwrecks.

Many consider wreck diving analogous to treasure hunting. While the latter has a universal appeal, it is usually unrewarding if the measure of success is money or jewels. For the most part, divers find more commonplace relics called artifacts. They too are treasures—treasures in and of history.

Wreck diving has fostered archaeological and historical research, as well as garnered artifacts from vessels that have for decades or even centuries rested at the bottom of the sea. The recovery, identification, dating and preservation of these historical objects have attracted both amateur and professional archaeologists. The preservation, however, of such artifacts can pose a major problem, and the amateur should know something of the difficulties and expense involved.

There is controversy regarding whether sport divers are "ripping off" historical wrecks. Except for a few in relatively protected areas, the ravages of time are slowly destroying underwater wrecks that may be lost (with their artifacts) for all time. The sea is cruel to all that does not belong in it. Even steel wrecks cannot withstand the combined forces of winds, waves, currents and corrosion.

*A word to the wise: it is extremely important that divers check with the appropriate state agency to familiarize themselves with shipwreck legislation and other restrictions.*

In the absence of natural reefs in New England it is interesting that man, albeit accidentally, has provided the basis for fascinating ecosystems—shipwrecks. It is stunning to see, for the first time, the incredible abundance, beauty, and diversity of marine life that has taken up residence in or around those sunken ships. On some wrecks, this growth of marine organisms is so dense that it completely obscures the structures of the vessel.

New England's shipwrecks are often beautiful and always fascinating for the sport diver; however, they may be hazardous. The entangling monofilament of lost fishing lines is one hazard encountered by wreck divers. It is the main reason for carrying a diving knife. Penetrating wrecks, especially deep ones, can be hazardous and divers need to observe certain safety rules. Dives requiring decompression stops add complications and danger. Another potential hazard is the large tidal fluctuation of Northern New England that usually produces strong currents. Some of the wrecks are located in that strong tidal zone.

Even shallow wrecks may be dangerous. Waves breaking over and around inshore wrecks can create a surge that will alternately push and pull. The sudden loss of control can throw a diver into jagged metal or other dangerous objects. Such diving is especially hazardous when visibility is poor. Divers seldom agree on visibility; one will claim that it is 10 feet and the next diver to surface will say it is 40 feet. This much is sure: excellent visibility is seldom encountered in New England waters and 20 feet is considered to be good. Visibility is usually better when the bottom is rock, gravel or sand because light is reflected. A mud and silt bottom absorbs light and can be easily disturbed by a diver or currents, further reducing visibility.

Yet, wreck diving can be safe with proper training, equipment and procedures. Do not attempt it without thorough professional preparation. Wreck diving certification is not required by wreck-diving charter boats, but basic certification is. Wreck diving, however, is no place for a beginner. Any inexperienced diver should contact his local dive shop to register for a Wreck Diving Certification course. Even the experienced wreck diver should proceed in graduated steps to the deeper more dangerous wrecks.

Shore access to shallow wrecks is limited because adjacent property is usually privately owned, and in northern New England the rocky terrain is often treacherous. In the 1960's and early 70's, it was difficult for a diver to get to the offshore wrecks, for there were few boat captains willing to take divers to these sites. Today, many dive charter boats are available to accommodate 6 to 40 divers at a time. Appendix A lists many of those boats. Also, local dive shops will provide dive charter information.

When you become experienced as a wreck diver in cold New England waters, with its poor visibility, you will feel confident and comfortable diving shipwrecks anywhere in the world.

H. Keatts

# Table of Contents

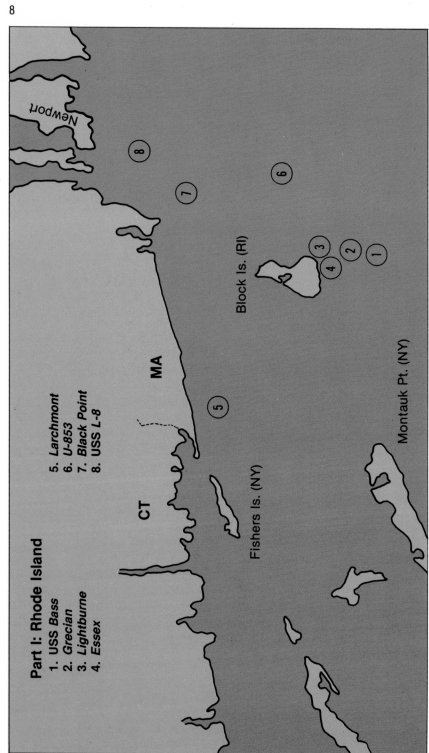

Part I: Rhode Island

1. USS Bass
2. Grecian
3. Lightburne
4. Essex
5. Larchmont
6. U-853
7. Black Point
8. USS L-8

Newport

CT

MA

Fishers Is. (NY)

Block Is. (RI)

Montauk Pt. (NY)

# 1. Test Target—USS *Bass*

| | | |
|---|---|---|
| **Type of vessel** | : | submarine |
| **Surface tons** | : | 2,620 |
| **Length** | : | 341.5 feet |
| **Beam** | : | 27.6 feet |
| **Hull construction** | : | steel |
| **Location** | : | 8.2 miles S of Block Island, RI |
| **Lat. and long.** | : | 41-01.09 N, 71-32.50 W |
| **Approximate depth of water:** | | 155 feet |

The United States submarine *Bass* (SS-*164*) owed her existence to the effective blockade maintained by the British over German merchant shipping during World War I. Desperate for critical war materials, the Germans devised a plan to run the blockade by underwater shipping aboard large freight-carrying U-boats. On July 9, 1916 the first of those underwater merchant vessels electrified the world with the first trans-Atlantic crossing by a submarine. Arrival of Germany's freight-carrying submarine *Deutschland* at Baltimore, Maryland stirred consternation in American defense circles. The demonstrated capability of U-boats to cross the ocean exposed the entire Eastern Seaboard to the potential for German military action.

The publicity did not escape attention by the U.S. Navy, concerned over the vast distances to be covered in fulfilling its commitments, particularly in the Pacific. The *Deutschland*'s success underlined the urgent need for larger, longer-range U.S. submarines. The merchant U-boats ultimately proved to be financially unsound, and the Germans converted them to combat U-boats—the same concept the U.S. Navy had in mind.

Military appropriations meet least opposition during wartime. Immediately after U.S. entry into World War I, a program was funded to develop an American version of Germany's merchant U-boats—but larger and with greater operating range. The development produced large submarines for the U.S. Navy—the V-class.

The second of the new vessels was launched at the Portsmouth (N.H.) Navy Yard in an impressive ceremony on December 27, 1924—not as the *Bass* but, in accordance with existing practice, as the *V-2*. The new submarine was more than twice the tonnage of the earlier S-class and had an operating range of over 12,000 miles. Armament included one three-inch gun, two machine guns, and six torpedo tubes, four forward and two aft, with 12 torpedoes.

After commissioning, *V-2*'s assignment was cruising the Atlantic coast and the Caribbean. She was transferred to San Diego in 1927 and, for the next ten years, the submarine operated along the Pacific coast, Hawaii, and again in the Caribbean. When the Navy changed submarine identification from numerical designations to types of fish on March 9, 1931 the *V-2* was renamed *Bass*, and four months later her designation was changed from

The *Bass* before her unsuccessful conversion to a cargo carrier. Note the famous shark-nosed bow. Photo courtesy of the Naval Historical Center.

SF-*5* to SS-*164*. The new class of submarine was a bitter disappointment. The main propulsion engines gave constant trouble, and when submerged the large submarines were difficult to maneuver.

In 1937, the submarine went into reserve after 13 years of peacetime service. Three years later, with the threat of war, she was recommissioned. In November, she sailed for the Canal Zone and served until hostilities broke out with Japan. She made four war patrols in 1942—but never encountered the enemy. However, a devastating fire in her aft battery room crippled the *Bass* as effectively as though she had been a combat victim. The spreading flames quickly engulfed the aft torpedo room and the starboard main motor room, consuming air and releasing toxic fumes. Asphyxiation claimed the lives of 25 enlisted men out of a crew of 80—a major disaster.

At the insistence of President Franklin Roosevelt, the *Bass*'s torpedo rooms and aft engine room were converted into cargo space. She was to be a cargo carrier like the *Deutschland* before her. However, like the German U-boat, she proved to be worthless in this role, and the *Bass* was designated to fill a humiliating role in a top-secret Navy operation as a passive target in the evaluation of air-borne anti-submarine weapons.

Although World War II was still in progress, the *Bass* was decommissioned, stripped, and designated a hulk on March 3, 1945, ending and inauspicous career. Her armament had been fired, but only in practice. The submarine's death knell sounded on March 18, 1945 when a skeleton crew sailed her to a point 8.2 miles south of Block Island, Rhode Island.

The *Bass* was left at anchor. A navy PBY-5A aircraft dropped two experimental Mark 24 torpex-filled mines which exploded, bringing a large boil of water and air to the surface. The submarine started to settle by the bow within 20 seconds; in less than a minute, the forward deck and conning tower were out of sight. The *Bass* continued to sink until her bow struck bottom, and the impact sheared the hull into two sections, just forward of

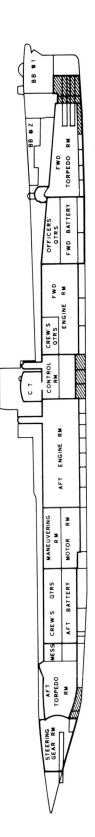

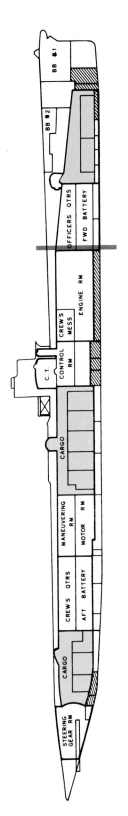

The submarine before, (above) and after (below) her conversion into a cargo carrier. The areas converted into cargo space are highlighted in yellow. Other new features include the cut-down conning tower and a peculiar "cigarette deck" aft of the conning tower. The red line shows where she broke in half when she struck the bottom. The diagram, before the highlighting was added, was taken from *The Fleet Submarine in the U.S. Navy*, by Commander John D. Alden. Copyright 1979, U.S. Naval Institute; printed by permission.

The sinking of the *Bass* by aircraft of the Anti-submarine Development Detachment. After an explosion off the stern, a large boil of water and air broke the surface to starboard and the submarine started to settle by the bow. Photo courtesy of the Naval Historical Center.

the conning tower. The stern slowly settled until, three minutes and forty seconds after the detonation, the target submarine disappeared.

No debris, only a few air bubbles that would soon be gone and residue from the torpex explosions, marked the grave of the *Bass*. The Navy's epitaph for the 20-year-old submarine that had never achieved its potential as a warship was appropriate in its brevity: "The rapid sinking of the hulk of the *Bass* indicates that the lethal characteristics of the Mark 24 mine are adequate."

The submarine, sitting upright on the white sand bottom, is not a dive for the average scuba diver because of the depth, approximately 140 feet to the deck, about 155 feet to the sand. Because of poor light penetration at that depth the dive often is a dark one. However, occasionally a diver swimming forward of the conning tower can view the broken off bow section—50 feet away. The hull break is just forward of a bulkhead, leaving the bow section open and easy to penetrate as far as the next bulkhead. Divers can also enter the forward engine room, where the hatch was removed. In this compartment there is very little room to maneuver because of the mass of machinery, and the diver may become disoriented and find it difficult to find the exit. Extreme caution is imperative when penetrating any wreck, especially the close quarters of a submarine.

This is one of the best shipwrecks in New England, but because of the 155-foot depth it is for experienced wreck divers only. At that depth everything becomes more complex, and the diver has little bottom time. Possible hazards include the bends, narcosis, carbon dioxide build-up, breathing resistance and loss of air supply. Careful planning and self-discipline are essential to ensure a safe dive.

Divers removed seven portholes from the anemone-covered conning tower. Carole Keatts looks through an empty port into the submarine's interior. Photo by the author.

The compass binnacle, on top of the conning tower, was unbolted and recovered by George Hoffman. When he opened the binnacle he found that the compass had been removed by Navy personnel. Photo by Tom Roach.

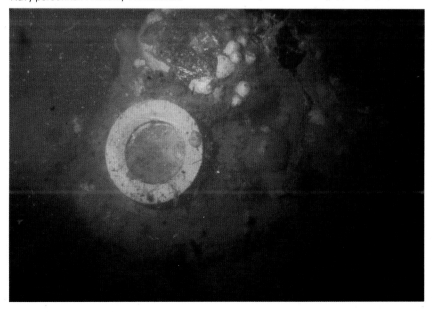

Dennis Kessler entering the oval hatch in the conning tower. The portholes are above him, and to his left is the pedestal for the 20mm anti-aircraft guns. Photo by Brad Sheard.

A series of submarine disasters stimulated designers to incorporate new features that would enable crewmen to escape. The *Bass* was given an unusual hull feature: a forward torpedo room hatch structure that combined the torpedo loading opening and escape hatch in a single casting. Photo by Bill Campbell.

The submarine's aft torpedo room was converted to cargo space. The hatch has not been opened. Photo by Brad Sheard.

The submarine was identified by divers penetrating the wreck in 1966, when they recovered a white wooden box containing an electrical armature with "U.S.S. Bass" stenciled in black on the side. A mattress and springs can be seen above the box. Photo by Michael A. deCamp.

Surprisingly, two manganese bronze, three-bladed, eight-foot-diameter screws have not been removed by salvors. Photo by Brad Sheard.

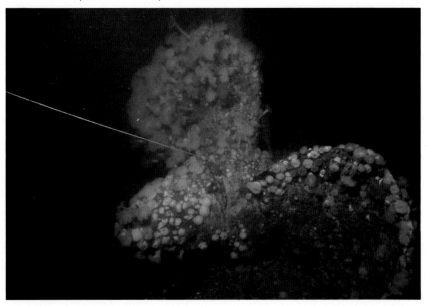

## 2. Collision in the Fog—*Grecian*

| | | |
|---|---|---|
| **Type of vessel** | : | freighter |
| **Gross tons** | : | 2,827 |
| **Length** | : | 290 feet |
| **Beam** | : | 42 feet |
| **Hull construction** | : | steel |
| **Location** | : | 3 miles S of Block Island's southeast point |
| **Lat. and long.** | : | 41-04.35 N, 71-32.14 W |
| **Approximate depth of water:** | | 90 feet |

The effort to launch the three-deck freight and passenger liner *Grecian* on December 30, 1899 was a miserable failure and an omen of bad luck for the Winsor Line steamer. She had been built at the Harlan & Hollingsworth Shipyards at Wilmington, Delaware.

When the blocks were sawed away and the ship started her plunge into the icy water, Miss Winsor, daughter of the president of the company, broke the traditional bottle of wine and christened the ship. To everyone's surprise and dismay, the *Grecian* moved only about 18 inches, then stuck. Investigation showed that the tallow, used to grease the ways, had frozen and caked. When the vessel started to move, the frozen tallow dropped from the ways and the ship rested on ungreased timbers.

Jacks were used to start the ship again, but an hour of hard work did not budge her. The liner was then shored up and made fast. The following day, with a new supply of tallow on the ways, the *Grecian* was successfully launched.

The *Grecian* was built in 1899 as a passenger liner with accommodations for 100 passengers. She was later converted into a freighter. Photo courtesy of The Mariners' Museum, Newport News, Virginia.

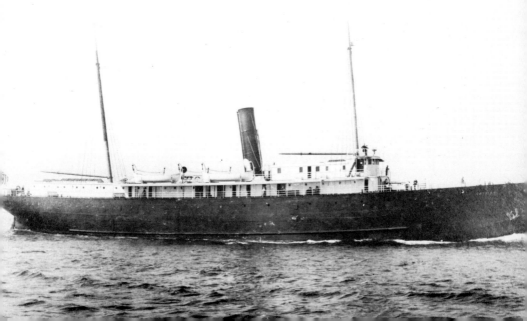

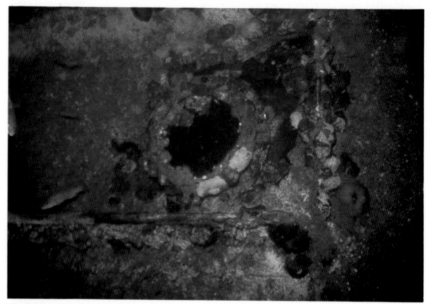

The bow, with its hawser opening, is the most intact part of the wreck. Photo by Chip Cooper.

The new ship had a steel deck house, with accommodations for about 100 passengers. She had four water-tight bulkheads, four hatches, four ports on each side and two steel masts. The *Grecian* was powered by triple-expansion engines with four boilers.

By Spring of 1932 the old steamer was no longer in the business of transporting passengers. She functioned only as a freighter, owned and operated by the Merchants and Miners Transportation Company, based in Baltimore, Maryland.

On the evening of May 26, the *Grecian* left Boston with a general cargo bound for Baltimore and Norfolk, Virginia. Her cargo of leather goods, molasses, printers ink, locks, shotguns and assorted goods was valued at $400,000, $100,000 more than the old ship.

The *Grecian* had made the run many times, but early the following morning she encountered fog southeast of Block Island, Rhode Island. Her captain reduced speed to 10 1/2 knots as a safety precaution. As the freighter steamed through the peasoup fog, the captain heard the fog signal of another vessel. Uncertain of the direction the sound came from, he ordered the engines stopped and the wheel put to port. Then he started ahead at slow speed. Almost immediately, the fog signal sounded again; this time he realized it was off his port bow. He ordered full speed astern.

To his horror, the lights of another ship, traveling very fast, appeared out of the fog. Two minutes later, the passenger liner *City of Chattanooga* cut into the port side of the *Grecian* just aft of the smokestack with what seemed to be slight impact. The liner had also been put into full speed astern, but she was still moving forward and cut into the freighter and remained lodged there.

The *Grecian* remained impaled on the liner's bow for about 13 minutes; then, filling with water, she pulled away and sank about three miles south of Block Island's Southeast Point Lighthouse.

The *City of Chattanooga*'s crew lowered lifeboats minutes after the collision and rescued 30 survivors from the *Grecian*. Four of the freighter's crew were never found and may have died in the collision, gone down with the ship, or were lost in the thick fog.

It was decided the *City of Chattanooga*, of the Savannah Line, had been at fault in the disaster. When her master first sighted the *Grecian* he ordered her wheel to starboard. If the wheel had been turned to port, the collision might have been avoided. It was also decided that the liner's speed was excessive for the existing conditions. Luckily, none of her crew of 29 and 85 passengers bound from Boston to New York were injured.

The bulk of the *Grecian*'s cargo was salvaged during the summers of 1932–33. She was then blown apart to reduce her potential as a hazard to other ships.

Visibility is usually good, often exceeding 40 feet. The bow is more intact than the rest of the ship, which is scattered over the white sand bottom in about 90 feet of water. The freighter's four large boilers make an impressive sight. Goosefish are frequently encountered on the wreck, so caution should be exercised when settling onto the sand bottom.

Many species of fish are found in, around, and on a wreck, and one minor hazard for wreck divers is the anglerfish or goosefish (*Lophius americanus*). This grotesque fish is a slow swimmer and lies camouflaged on the bottom while dangling its lure (a modified dorsal fin) to attract its prey. It has an enormous mouth with many slender, sharp, inward-curving teeth, as much as an inch long in larger specimens. They can grow to four feet long and weigh as much as 50 pounds. Photo by the author.

Divers find many brass artifacts on the *Grecian*. The valve above was photographed, recovered and preserved (below) by Chip Cooper.

# 3. Lost at Lighthouse—*Lightburne*

| | | |
|---|---|---|
| **Type of vessel** | : | tanker |
| **Gross tons** | : | 6,429 |
| **Length** | : | 431.6 feet |
| **Beam** | : | 56 feet |
| **Hull construction** | : | steel |
| **Location** | : | Block Island's southeast point |
| **Lat. and long.** | : | 41-08.58 N, 71-32.54 W |
| **Approximate depth of water:** | | 15–25 feet |

"North Atlantic Paradise" and "Bermuda of the North" are two names frequently used to describe a small island off the Rhode Island coast. The native Indians called this pork chop-shaped island Manisses, which meant "Isle of the Little God." In 1614 a Dutch explorer, Captain Adrian Block, gave his name to the island.

Today Block Island is a popular summer resort, but for a couple of centuries it has been a stumbling block for maritime commerce. The island, seven miles in length, is astride the heavily traveled trade route between New York and Boston.

The glacier that formed Block Island 10,000 years ago dumped many large boulders along the south, east and west shores. Scattered among the boulders are the remains of many shipwrecks—disasters that over the years have presented the isolated Islanders with many essentials and a few luxuries.

The waters around Block Island are notorious for dense fog that seems to develop within minutes on some occasions. As an aid to mariners, a lighthouse was built on the island's southeast point in 1874–75. The lighthouse, however, was of no aid to the Texaco tanker *Lightburne* when she encountered dense fog southwest of Block Island en route from Port Arthur, Texas to Providence, Rhode Island.

The Texaco tanker *Lightburne* was built in 1919 at Bath, Maine. Photo courtesy of Bob Cartier.

In 1939, the tanker grounded in front of Block Island's Southeast Point Lighthouse. Photo courtesy of Paul C. Morris.

At 7:30 p.m. on February 10 the *Lightburne*, carrying 72,000 barrels of gasoline and kerosene, went aground on the rocky shoals directly in front of the lighthouse. Captain Alexander Wolman sent out an SOS followed by a report that his ship's engine room was flooded and the tanker was in danger of breaking up. The *Lightburne* was being pounded badly by a heavy sea, and it was impossible to launch lifeboats.

The Coast Guard Station at New London picked up the SOS and relayed it to the Point Judith Station, which transmitted the message by radio to the Coast Guard Unit at Block Island.

While the Coast Guard cutters *Campbell* and *Active* from New London and several other vessels, including the SS *Oakey L. Alexander* (see episode 29), were headed to the scene, four members of the Block Island Coast Guard Unit launched a 36-foot motor lifeboat and started on the 10-mile trip around the island.

The *Oakey L. Alexander* and another ship reached the general area of the disaster first, but could not make contact because of the dense fog. Captain Wolman radioed he could hear their whistles but could not see them. Also, he reported that his ship was bouncing heavily on the rocks, waves were sweeping over the tanker's decks, and he and his crew were in a precarious position.

Shortly followed another message: "Master wants every ship near him to come to his assistance immediately." The search intensified. It was followed by ". . .*Lightburne* may break up at any minute." Although the potential rescue vessels could hear the tanker's bell, the fog discouraged them from venturing into the shallow water.

Two-and-one-half hours after the *Lightburne* grounded, the Block Island lifeboat found the tanker and removed 16 of the 37-man crew. The lifeboat, braving pounding seas, had maneuvered leeward of the tanker, which was pitched so far onto her port side that the 16 men simply stepped off into the rescue vessel. The lifeboat came alongside the cutter *Active* but, due to a 35-knot wind, the water was too rough to make a transfer, so the 16 men were put ashore at Old Harbor about 11 p.m.

The lifeboat, making a slow journey through the rough sea, returned to the grounded tanker and removed the remaining 21 men and Trixie, the *Lightburne*'s canine mascot for 13 years. This time they successfully transferred the men to the cutter.

The *Lightburne* was equipped with a radio compass and direction finder, so that her course could be plotted with absolute precision by using the three nearest land radio stations as coordinates—in this case Montauk, Block Island, and Nantucket. Captain Wolman attributed the grounding of his ship to strong southeast winds, heavy groundswell, and dense fog.

The *Lightburne*'s crew was ordered to remain on Block Island until the underwriters had investigated the disaster. Hotels and cottages, closed for the season, were opened to accommodate the 37-man crew. Eleven officers and crew were quartered at Ballard's Inn.

The day after the tanker grounded she was threatened by another menace—fire. About 24,000 barrels of gasoline had leaked from her punctured hull. When the motion of a heavy sea dislodged an automatic flare life-buoy from the ship's rail, the gasoline-covered water ignited with a roar and a column of smoke and flame shot 150 feet into the sky. The wind, blowing from the northwest, forced the flames out to sea, away from the threatened tanker. The wind quickly split the flames into two sheets of fire, that burned for an hour and a half. The following day the *Lightburne*'s crew returned to salvage clothing and belongings they had left behind when they were rescued.

The *Lightburne* was built in 1919 at Bath, Maine. Although the tanker had been in service for 20 years, Texaco, Incorporated wanted to save the ship. Merritt, Chapman & Scott, a salvage company, was contracted to refloat the *Lightburne*. Some petroleum was removed, but the incessant pounding on the rocks for several days split the tanker's hull and the wreck was declared a total loss.

An investigating board of the Bureau of Marine Inspection and Navigation filed formal charges of negligence against Captain Wolman. The board faulted him for not taking adequate precautions in bad weather conditions as his ship approached Providence.

Block Island residents salvaged many useful items from the tanker. Fred Benson and another Islander visited the wreck several months after she grounded. Fred opened a hatch and found kerosene. Seawater had leaked into the hold, but the kerosene was floating on top. The two men went ashore and returned with barrels and a bucket. They skimmed off the kerosene with the bucket, filled the barrels, and shared their find with

Several days of constant pounding on the rocks split the *Lightburne*'s hull and the wreck was declared a total loss. Photo courtesy of Bob Cartier.

other Islanders. Fred also discovered 400-pound barrels of asphalt that he sold in New Bedford.

The *Lightburne*'s two and one-half-ton anchor was recovered and sold to the U.S. Government. During World War II it was used to anchor Newport's anti-submarine net. A salvage company from Newport removed two four-bladed bronze screws, each blade weighing 4,200 pounds.

The wreck is covered with kelp and the frequent surge produces a beautiful sight—long tendrils of brown seaweed swaying back and forth with the water's flow. The surge, however, is a potential hazard that may propel a diver onto jagged or pointed pieces of steel wreckage. Visibility depends on the strength of the surge which determines the amount of sand suspended in the water.

On a calm day the wreck is easy to find. The site is marked with a buoy about 400 feet on the seaward side. Wreckage is scattered in 15 to 25 feet of water and several large pieces are near the surface at low tide. The bow is more intact. The wreckage when viewed from the surface appears dark against the white sand bottom. Divers with large boats must be cautious when approaching the wreck to avoid the same fate that sent the *Lightburne* to the bottom.

A diver looks into the more intact bow section. Photo by Chip Cooper.

Chip Cooper took this photo of a ladder from inside the wreck.

## 4. Mistake or Mishap—*Essex*

| | | |
|---|---|---|
| **Type of vessel** | : | freighter |
| **Gross tons** | : | 3,018 |
| **Length** | : | 272 feet |
| **Beam** | : | 40 feet |
| **Hull construction** | : | steel |
| **Location** | : | Block Island's southeast point |
| **Lat. and long.** | : | 41-08.47 N, 71-33.11 W |
| **Approximate depth of water:** | | 25–30 feet |

Two-and-one-half years after the *Lightburne* grounded off Block Island's Southeast Point Lighthouse, disaster struck again—almost at the same spot. On a clear, moonlit night, September 25, 1941, the lighthouse keeper stood in the yard enjoying the beautiful Fall weather. Although the light was on, flashing a warning to approaching ships, he watched in amazement as the freighter *Essex* crashed into the island, backed offshore and then grounded again.

Why did the freighter ground on a calm, clear, moonlit night, almost in front of a functioning lighthouse? The *Essex* had radioed she was taking water into her engine room and, shortly after the transmission, grounded to keep from sinking. The Coast Guard later speculated that she must have struck a floating object and holed her hull. If that were the case why did she run aground, pull offshore and then ground again? Some Islanders, includ-

The *Essex* was built in 1890 as a passenger liner with accommodations for 200 passengers. Fifty years later she was converted into a freighter. Photo courtesy of the Steamship Historical Society Collection, Univ. of Baltimore Library.

ing the lighthouse keeper, were of the opinion the freighter was running with no one on watch, and when she grounded the captain backed her off to check the damage. The ship's crew discovered she was leaking badly and in danger of sinking. Captain Harold Andersen radioed the Coast Guard that she was taking on water. Then to keep his ship from sinking, Andersen ordered her to be grounded a second time. Had the *Essex* been unlucky enough to strike a floating object, or was the accident because of crew negligence?

The *Essex* had been built in 1890 by the William Cramp & Sons' Ship and Engine Building Company of Philadelphia. She was built for the Merchants and Miners Transportation Company of Boston to carry passengers between that city and Baltimore. The steamer was equipped with four decks; the upper and main decks provided accommodations for 200 passengers. The *Essex* was fitted with triple expansion engines and four boilers. In the interest of economy the owners did not have blowers installed in the fire room. As a consequence, the temperature below averaged 120 to 135 degrees. Blowers would have reduced that to about 95 degrees. In addition to steam propulsion she was rigged as a two-masted schooner.

The *Essex* remained in service for Merchants and Miners for 50 years. The old steamer was sold to the White Pearl Shipping Corporation of New York in 1940. The new owners retained the steamer's name, but converted her to a freighter and modernized her for trans-Atlantic use. The *Essex* was on her first voyage for her new owners when she grounded on Block Island. The freighter was en route from Lisbon, Portugal to New York with a cargo of 600 tons of cork and 500 tons of sand ballast.

After grounding on the island the 41-man crew first refused to abandon the stranded steamer, which had 30 feet of water in her engine room. The *Essex* was in no danger of breaking up, but the crew agreed to board the Coast Guard cutter *Argo*. However, the captain and several others returned the following day and remained throughout the salvage operation.

Islanders were hired to man gasoline pumps in an attempt to remove water from the holds so that the ship could be refloated. One of the local men, Fred Benson, was working at the task when Captain Andersen noticed the water level had dropped four inches. The captain told Fred "we are gaining on it and we will be in New York in three days." However, as Fred noticed, the reason the water level had dropped was the tide was falling. When the tide changed Captain Andersen realized his mistake and summoned a professional diver from the mainland. The diver found extensive damage to the hull and the old steamer was declared a total loss. Fred Benson was asked to form a salvage crew to recover the cork cargo. Fred and his crew of 12 received $1.00 an hour, a bonanza to the Islanders.

Bales of cork were removed through the forward cargo hatch, the only deck hatch on the converted passenger ship. The cork was floating on the surface of the water-filled hold, wedged against the deck. The diver was ordered to work his way under the cork to another cargo hold. Forty-six years later, Fred declared that the owners were trying to recover something other than cork, but the diver could not find it. That cargo hold also contained 200-pound bags of almonds that turned the water ink black.

After removing the cork from the forward hold, the salvage crew cut through the deck over the aft cargo area. About 3,500 bales, 4.5 feet by 30 inches, were recovered. Lead showers, 100 pounds each, were removed from the heads. Many of the glass swing plates were removed from the portholes. The rims were left, because they were too difficult to remove. Steel plates had been welded over the hull openings to protect against damage from bullets during World War II. Although the United States was supposedly a neutral country when the plates were installed, American merchant ships were subject to attack by German U-boats. After almost 50 years of seawater corrosion, these porthole rims are still difficult to remove. The Islanders were allowed to scrap the recovered metal for which they received $400—a nice bonus for their hard work.

In December salvage work was halted when a southeaster hit the *Essex*, destroying the superstructure, ripping up deck planks, and washing the remaining cork onto the island. Bales were deposited 50 feet up the bluff.

Subsequent storms continued to break up the freighter, scattering her wreckage in 25 to 30 feet of water. The most recognizable features are the bow, the boilers and large steel plates and ribs. Shifting sand occasionally exposes an intact porthole or rim. Divers searching the rock-strewn sandy bottom are occasionally rewarded with artifacts from the freighter.

Visibility depends on the strength of the surge which determines the amount of sand suspended in the water.

Three months after grounding, a winter storm tore off the superstructure, ripped up much of the decking, washed away the remaining cork cargo and halted the salvage work after nearly half the cargo had been saved. Photo courtesy of Fred Benson.

Block Island's wrecking crew unload bales of cork from the salvage boat. Fred Benson, who allowed the author to use the photograph, is on the left.

The nautical chart of Block Island does not show a wreck symbol for the *Essex*, but the *Lightburne*, seen off the freighter's bow, is marked on the chart and gives an approximate location for the *Essex*. Photo courtesy of Fred Benson.

Cosmo Stoia swims over steel plates. Photo by Mike Casalino

Bill Palmer prepares to send this complete porthole to the surface with a lift bag. Photo by Bill Campbell.

## 5. New England's Worst Marine Disaster—*Larchmont*

| | | |
|---|---|---|
| **Type of vessel** | : | passenger liner |
| **Gross tons** | : | 1,605 |
| **Length** | : | 252.1 feet |
| **Beam** | : | 37 feet |
| **Hull construction** | : | wood |
| **Location** | : | 3 miles SE of Watch Hill, RI |
| **Lat. and long.** | : | 41-16.06 N, 71-49.18 W |
| **Approximate depth of water:** | | 140 feet |

In the annals of maritime history, many instances have occurred where the captain was the last to leave a sinking ship. A notable exception to this standard happened in New England's worst marine disaster, the sinking of the *Larchmont*.

Youthful Captain George W. McVay was accused of cowardice and being the first to leave his sinking ship. McVay was the second youngest to have commanded a Long Island Sound passenger vessel. When the disaster occurred he was only 26 years old and had been captain of the *Larchmont* for almost two years.

The *Cumberland* was built in 1885 for the International Line at Bath, Maine. The vessel had her share of problems. In 1902 she was in a collision in Boston Harbor and had to be run aground to save her. She was sold "as is" to the Joy Line for $60,000 and renamed the *Larchmont*, for a New York town located on Long Island Sound. The same year, under her new owners, she caught fire and her 200 passengers were panic-stricken, but the crew managed to extinguish the fire. Two years later she ran down the lumber-laden schooner *D.T. Melanson* and the same year she grounded twice. In 1905 the ship's crew had a difficult time saving the steamer from another fire, this time caused by defective insulation.

At 7 p.m. on February 11, 1907, the *Larchmont* left Providence, RI, for New York. The steamer was owned by the Joy Line but this passage would offer no joy to those on board: all except a few were on their last journey. It was never determined exactly how many were subjected to the horrors that were about to unfold. Nothing seems to have been learned from the *Portland*, which foundered in 1898, taking with her the only passenger list. The public had been in a furor because a duplicate had not been deposited with the marine authorities ashore. It has been reported that anywhere from 200 to 342 passengers and crew were aboard the *Larchmont*, and a large cargo of freight valued at $45,000 was on board. She was licensed to carry 600, but fortunately she was under-booked.

A strong northwest wind was blowing as the *Larchmont* steamed through the eastern passage of Narragansett Bay. A gale was blowing between 35 and 40 knots out in the Sound. However, its effect was not felt until she rounded Point Judith at 9:30 p.m. Then the side-wheeler pointed

When the passenger steamer *Larchmont* sank in a collision, the small deck house with five staterooms, beneath the stern mast, miracuously separated from the deck as the ship went under. Thirty-five passengers were precariously perched on top. Sketch courtesy of Fred Benson.

her bow into the very heart of the icy blast and continued through Block Island Sound until she was abeam of Watch Hill, within five or six miles of Fisher's Island.

About 11 p.m. the crew of a three-masted schooner, the *Harry Knowlton*, said they sighted the *Larchmont* steaming westward and admired the well-lighted side-wheeler. "Thats the life," one crewman said to another, "warm and comfortable in zero weather!"

The *Larchmont* was momentarily lost from sight because of the rough sea. Suddenly she appeared again, but now heading directly for the schooner. Captain Haley, expecting the steamer to turn and give his sailing vessel the right of way, ordered the helmsman to hold his course. At the last moment, the men in the *Larchmont*'s pilot house tried to turn and avoid a collision. It was too late. As the larger steamer was slowly veering around in response to her helm, the schooner, being pushed by the gale, crashed into the port side of the *Larchmont* just forward of the paddlebox.

The impact of the coal-laden schooner was so intense that its bow cut its way more than half-way across the steamer's 37-foot beam. With the force of the impact spent, the schooner was temporarily held fast to the stricken *Larchmont*. At least for a moment, the water was held in check. Unfortunately, the pounding sea soon separated the vessels, and water rushed into the gaping hole in the steamer's hull. Water poured over the cargo and down into the hold.

During the collision the main steam line was cut, stopping the engines and enveloping the *Larchmont* with clouds of scalding steam, adding to the confusion. Panic-stricken passengers, many of whom had been thrown

The 128-foot, coal-laden schooner *Harry Knowlton* rammed the *Larchmont*. Although the steamer was twice her size, the schooner's captain managed to beach her without loss of life near Watch Hill, R.I. Photo courtesy of The Mariners' Museum, Newport News, Virginia.

from their bunks when the collision occurred, were at first under the impression that a fire had started on board.

The agonizing ordeal of the passengers who had not been scalded to death, crushed or drowned in their staterooms was about to begin. Few had dressed before rushing to the decks. Most were in night clothes. Their fear overcame the bitter cold, about zero, and the first penetrating blasts of the gale. Suffering from the elements intensified, but those who had not stopped to dress properly now found it impossible to return to their staterooms that were already flooded.

Captain McVay ordered the ship to be abandoned. Later he stated, "My boat was the last to leave the ship, as nearly as I can determine, although I could not tell accurately what took place on the other side of the vessel. . . ." The lifeboat contained only eight persons including McVay; none were passengers.

"I saw at once," reported McVay, "that the wind and sea were against our getting to Watch Hill and consequently gave orders that the crew should circle the *Larchmont* in hope of picking up some of the passengers. We tried this, but found that the sea and wind were too much for us, and after what seemed to us like an age we had to give up the job. . . . The majority of the passengers were on the leeward side of the vessel. That was the side which was highest in the water. . . . All I know was that the passengers piled into the boats as well as they could. . . ." It is apparent by his own statement that most of the passengers able to reach the deck were still on board when McVay launched his lifeboat with only eight occupants.

The *Larchmont* settled on an even keel and sank out of sight about 15 minutes after the collision. As the steamer went down, the row of staterooms on the Hurricane Deck miracuously separated from the deck and floated, with about 35 people perched on top. They were soon covered with ice, and the small deckhouse was pitched around, driven by the storm-driven waves.

The following morning, a Captain Smith in the small fishing schooner *Elsie* put out from Block Island in search of survivors. When Captain Smith sighted the ice-encrusted deckhouse four miles north of Block Island at 11 a.m., only 16 persons remained upon it. Eight of them were dead. Two survivors were women, the only females to survive the *Larchmont* disaster. In the 12 hours that the deckhouse had been tossed about by the sea, most of its human cargo had died of exposure and slid into the sea one by one. The deckhouse eventually grounded on Sandy Point, Block Island.

The experience was the same for those fortunate, or unfortunate, enough to find a place in a lifeboat. Most suffered slow death by freezing. Every wave, crashing against the open boats, sent spray over the occupants until a coating of ice enveloped everyone. The ordeal of reaching land was terrible. The metal lifeboats were heavy and the oars covered with ice. Captain McVay said: "It was bitter cold and the cold was so intense that it was almost impossible to do anything but drift before the wind. . . ." He was in the first lifeboat to come ashore. It was 6:30 a.m. at Sandy Point on

The deckhouse, which allowed eight passengers to survive the disaster, washed ashore at Sandy Point, Block Island. This section of the Hurricane Deck was used as a fisherman's shanty for many years. Photo courtesy of Fred Benson.

the northwest shore of Block Island. Not a man on board could walk. Their feet were frozen so badly that they had to be carried 300 yards from the beach to the lifesaving station.

Apparently only three of eight lifeboats reached land. The other five and four liferafts were probably never launched. The 560 cork life preservers the *Larchmont* carried were useless in the bitter cold water.

News of the disaster swiftly spread across Block Island and within two or three hours, every inhabitant was at the beach, braving the still-blowing gale to help survivors. However, there was too few survivors. The major task was hauling bodies out of the surf as they washed ashore. When darkness settled over the island that night, 45 frozen dead had been recovered from the surf or from the boats which drifted ashore. Those bodies, encrusted with ice, were lined up in the lifesaving stations.

The sea cast bodies and wreckage on the shore for days. The Joy Line steamer *Kentucky* was sent to Block Island to pick up the survivors and the bodies of 70 dead. Only 19 of the passengers and crew on board the *Larchmont* reached land alive, and two died from their ordeal within several days. Of the initial 19 survivors, 10 were from the crew of 52. Only nine were passengers. In 1950, the *Larchmont*'s Quartermaster, James E. Staples, wrote a report that 332 perished in the disaster. Although no one knows for certain how many died, it was undoubtedly New England's worst.

McVay had said that, as nearly as he could determine, his lifeboat was the last to leave the ship. In answer to the charge of a witness, he said that

Forty-five ice-encrusted bodies, victims of the *Larchmont* disaster, were recovered and lined up in Block Island lifesaving stations. Photo courtesy of the Block Island Historical Society.

his boat went into the water first, but he waited around the sinking steamer until she sank, doing what he could to save passengers.

In a *New York Times* editorial of February 14, 1907, it is said of McVay: "He was cool enough. Without delay he ascertained the extent of the damage his vessel had sustained, and when he realized the hopelessness of the situation he gave the proper and necessary orders for equipping and launching the boats. But for the execution of these orders, he says himself, he trusted to his officers and crew, and his own attention seems to have been devoted to manning and getting into the water what he calls his own boat. . . ."

The following day the same newspaper ran an editorial including the following: "Captain McVay of the lost *Larchmont* does not seem in the least. . . to apprehend the ethics of the seafaring profession, or that it has any. . . . He explains that it was by his foresight in securing the 'best crew' for 'his own boat' that he was able to get away first from his sinking ship. And, really, he seems to think that is all there is to it . . . the point of honor is that the Captain of a ship must make sure that all his passengers are saved before he makes an effort to save himself. . . ."

An official inquiry by United States Steamboat Inspectors was held at New London. McVay testified that he had not helped the passengers, saying that because of the steamer's rapid sinking he had not had time to "chase around."

The inquiry into the disaster lasted two months. The Inspectors held that the collision resulted from "careless and unskillful navigation on the part of the pilot of the *Larchmont*, John L. Anson." The dead pilot, a victim of the disaster, had violated a basic rule of the sea: steam vessels should give the right of way to sailing vessels. Surprisingly, the Inspectors said they lacked enough evidence to charge Captain McVay with incompetence or misconduct.

The wreck is approximately three-and-one-half miles southeast of Watch Hill, RI, in about 140 feet of water. Diving on the *Larchmont* should be done only at slack tide. Currents to three and four knots are common. Divers should go down and come back up the anchor line. The wreck site is in the shipping lane and if a diver surfaces away from the boat with the current starting to "run," he can be quickly carried away. Not only because of the current, but also because this is a "black water" dive, it is a good idea to use a safety line attached to the anchor line. Once the diver goes below about 70 feet there is very little light penetration and it is extremely dark. Dive lights are a must.

Fishing nets on the wreck can be a danger at anytime because of the poor visibility, but when a current is running they are a very serious hazard.

The wreckage is scattered, but both massive paddle-wheels extend up 70 feet from the bottom. By looking and digging under the decking, many artifacts, such as silverware, china, and portholes, can be recovered.

The massive paddle-wheels, extending up 70 feet from the bottom, are an impressive sight. The upper photo, by Brian Skerry, was taken close to the wheel's hub, while the lower photo, by Bill Campbell, shows a trawler's met draped on the top of the wheel.

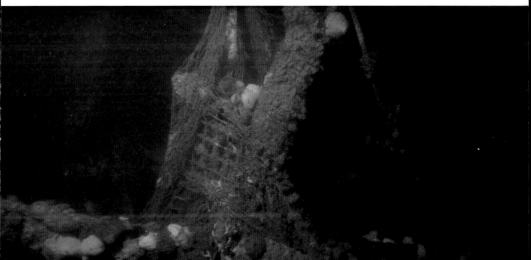

Wreckage strewn about the bottom. Photo by Bill Campbell.

The side-wheeler was built in 1885 for the International Line and sold to the Joy Line 17 years later. A porthole and plate recovered from the wreck by Bill Palmer. The china has the International Line insignia. Photo by Bill Campbell.

# 6. Last Kill in American Waters—*U-853*

| | | |
|---|---|---|
| **Type of vessel** | : | submarine |
| **Surface tons** | : | 740 |
| **Length** | : | 251.9 feet |
| **Beam** | : | 22.5 feet |
| **Hull construction** | : | steel |
| **Location** | : | 7 miles east of Block Island, RI |
| **Lat. and long.** | : | 41-14.3 N, 71-25.2 W |
| **Approximate depth of water:** | | 130 feet |

The nautical chart of Rhode Island Sound features a circle seven miles east of Block Island, Rhode Island labeled "Danger, unexploded depth charge, May 1945." That cryptic monument to the last sea action between the U.S. and Nazi Germany marks the sandy grave of German U-boat *U-853*. Her story tells the end of a struggle for an ocean; her death serves as the knell for the end of a war.

One of the most decisive military conflicts in the history of warfare was termed by Winston Churchill the "Battle of the Atlantic," the confrontation that pitted Germany's World War II submarine fleet against Britain, Canada and the United States. He wrote in *The Second World War*: "The only thing that ever really frightened me during the war was the U-boat peril. . . . I was even more anxious about this battle than I had been about the glorious air fight called the Battle of Britain."

The *U-853*, a Type IXC U-boat, was commissioned on June 25, 1943. She spent the next few months on a shake-down cruise in the Baltic. On April 29, 1944 the submarine left Kiel, Germany for her first war mission.

The *U-853* and four other U-boats had been assigned to the mid-Atlantic between Newfoundland and the Azores to make weather observations for the defense of the European Continent. With such information, German Intelligence believed it could anticipate Allied invasion plans across the English Channel, which would be influenced heavily by weather conditions.

Although the meterological mission was not as dangerous as attacking an escorted convoy, it was still risky. Each U-boat had a meterologist on board and had to surface daily for weather observations and to transmit the conditions by radio. Every message provided Allied units in the Atlantic with the opportunity for a radio-directional fix on the surfaced U-boat.

While surfaced for a weather transmission, the *U-853* was strafed by Allied fighter planes. Two of the crew were killed, several others wounded. The captain was riddled by slugs and fragments that ripped into his head, stomach, and arms. He suffered 28 wounds. The U-boat returned to her base in Lorient, France.

On February 24, 1945 the *U-853* slipped out of Stavanger, Norway, one of Germany's alternative operational centers, and headed across the Atlantic for the New England Coast—this time never to return.

*U-853* entering a French port. The submarine holds the dubious distinction of being the last U-boat to be sunk in American waters. Photo courtesy of Fred Benson.

The war in Europe was quickly being brought to a close. Several German armies in Northern Europe were scheduled to surrender on May 5 at 8 a.m. European time. Though Field-Marshall Montgomery had accepted an armistice for German forces in northwest Europe, General Eisenhower declined the armistice until a general capitulation included the Russian front.

On the night of May 4, Admiral Doenitz, Head of State following Hitler's suicide, broadcast the following order: "All U-boats. Cease fire at once. Stop all hostile action against Allied shipping. Doenitz." There is no record that the *U-853* acknowledged receipt of that order.

During the afternoon of May 5, the U-boat was cruising at periscope depth east of Block Island. Scanning the seas by periscope, her captain sighted two freighters, a tanker, a tug hauling three barges, and the small collier *Black Point*, a 5,353-ton, 27-year-old coal carrier which probably would have been scrapped if the war had not forced to sea practically everything that could float. Yet, that unattractive relic was to fall victim to the marauding U-boat.

The *Black Point* was entering the western end of Rhode Island Sound, four miles southeast of Point Judith, at 5:40 p.m. Without warning, a torpedo explosion tore away 40 feet of her stern. The *Black Point* sunk fast by what was left of her stern (see episode 7).

The crew of a nearby Yugoslav freighter witnessed the action. Two minutes later, an SOS was sent out warning of a U-boat in the area. Unfortunately for the *U-853*, part of a U.S. Navy Task Force was only 30 miles away, en route to the Boston Navy Yard for repairs and provisions.

As dusk fell, the U-boat was resting quietly on the sandy bottom. She had been in tight spots before and had always eluded her hunters. However, this time she had ventured into shallow coastal waters and enemy warships were bearing down on her. In deeper water, the *U-853* would have had a chance to escape, but a submarine cornered in shallow water has little chance because sonar can pinpoint her location more readily and she is an easier target for depth charges.

The destroyer escort *Atherton* located the *U-853* less than three hours after the *Black Point*'s sinking. The attack began at 8:29 p.m., but the U-boat was not declared "sunk and on the bottom" until 10:45 the next morning.

Practice attacks continued until 12:24 p.m. Nine hours and 17 minutes after the last depth charge was dropped on the *U-853*, German Chief-of-Staff General Jodl and Admiral Friedeburg, Doenitz' friend and personal representative, signed unconditional surrender papers at Reims, France. There were no survivors, and today the *U-853* is the underwater tomb of her crew.

U.S. Navy divers were ordered to penetrate the U-boat and recover papers from the captain's safe. They were unsuccessful, and the effort was

The U-boat's crew at the commissioning exercises. Photo courtesy of Fred Benson.

abandoned when it was reported that at least 12 unexploded depth charges were strewn around the *U-853*.

Eight years passed before anyone visited the U-boat. Then, between 1953 and 1960, a rash of diving activity was stimulated by rumors that the *U-853* was not on a marauding mission when she was destroyed. Instead, she was reported to have carried an exotic cargo ranging from a treasure of gold bullion to flasks of mercury and American currency. It was even rumored that the U-boat was to serve as Hitler's get-away boat.

Nothing came of the salvage efforts, and the *U-853* still rests in her sandy grave. However, salvage attempts have continued, as recently as 1981. Those efforts have undoubtedly been stimulated by the many stories of the U-boat's mission and cargo that persist even today.

The *U-853* is one of the most popular dive sites in New England, regularly visited by sport divers. The U-boat lies seven miles due east of Block Island in about 130 feet of water, sitting upright on the sandy bottom.

The pressure hull was originally enclosed by a thin steel envelope, designed to streamline the U-boat. The corrosive effects of years under the sea have removed most of that outer covering. The wooden decking is gone, exposing a mass of tangled gridwork and pipes. The conning tower does not look as one might expect, because the streamlined outer envelope corroded away long ago and the upper part of the periscope was cut off.

Side scan sonar printout of the *U-853*. Courtesy of EG & G.

Only the conning tower's pressure hull and periscope stalk remain.

Several open deck hatches invite the curious to explore the *U-853*'s interior compartments. The conning tower hatch cover has been removed and a diver can enter easily with a single tank. Because of the extensive damage caused by the Navy's furious attack, there are several other places for divers to enter the hull. Forward of the conning tower, the pressure hull is blown open and a diver with a set of double air tanks can easily enter through the gaping hole. From that point, the diver can pass through a circular hatch and enter the control room, which appeared quite different in 1945 than it does today. The compartment contained most of the principal controls for operating the U-boat, but massive deterioration has occurred and divers have removed most of the gauges and instruments.

The 37mm anti-aircraft gun on the U-boat's stern, designed to fire 100 shells a minute, was a photographer's delight until the gun barrel and flak shield were accidentally torn off by a salvage boat's mooring line. A Navy anchor that was used to grapple for the U-boat still lies in the sand on the starboard side, with the anchor chain draped over the conning tower.

It is a thoughtful experience to dive the *U-853*, the last U-boat to have been sunk in U.S. waters during the Second World War, and to follow with a dive on her victim, the *Black Point*, the last ship to be torpedoed off the coast of the U.S. in World War II.

Carole Keatts swims past the 37mm anti-aircraft gun on the U-boat's stern. In 1981 the barrel and flak shield were accidentally torn off by a salvage boat's mooring line. Photo by Mike Casalino.

Forward torpedo room showing a torpedo tube door decorated with a woman's name, Hannelore. The C clamp is one of four installed during a salvage attempt 20 years after the U-boat was sunk. Photo by the author.

The fins on the end of a torpedo in the *U-853*'s forward torpedo room. Photo by the author.

# 7. Last Ship Sunk in American Waters by a U-Boat—
## *Black Point*

| | | |
|---|---|---|
| **Type of vessel** | : | collier |
| **Gross tons** | : | 5,353 |
| **Length** | : | 368 feet |
| **Beam** | : | 55 feet |
| **Hull construction** | : | steel |
| **Location** | : | 3 1/2 miles SE of Pt. Judith Lighthouse |
| **Lat. and long.** | : | 41-19.02 N, 71-25.01 W |
| **Approximate depth of water:** | | bow 95 feet, stern 85 feet |

The ancient collier (coal hauling vessel) holds the dubious distinction of being the last ship sunk in American waters by Hitler's U-boats during the Second World War.

The *Black Point*, with 7,595 tons of coal in her holds, had run from Norfolk, Virginia to New York in convoy. From New York, traveling alone, she had taken the "safe" passage through Long Island Sound. The Island protected her from U-boats that might be prowling in the Atlantic. The collier had made it across the open waters of Block Island Sound without incident. Another short run of about 30 nautical miles and she would reach the comparative safety of Buzzard's Bay and the approaches to Cape Cod Canal.

The *Black Point*, the last ship sunk by U-boat action in American waters during the Second World War, was a victim of *U-853*. Photo courtesy of the National Archives.

The *Black Point* was peacefully entering the western end of Rhode Island Sound, about three-and-one-half miles southeast of Point Judith, Rhode Island, on the afternoon of May 5, 1945. Even though they had been warned of U-boat activity, within a few miles of the Newport Navy Base the collier's officers must have felt safe, because the ship was not following the anti-submarine defense of zigzagging. Her captain had just finished his dinner and had returned to the bridge. He was lighting a cigarette when, without warning, a torpedo explosion tore away 40 feet of her stern. The explosion produced heavy concussion, causing the glass faces of clocks and gauges to shatter and fly through the air, and a terrific billow of ashes, smoke, and soot emerged from the stack. The mainmast was blown over the port side and both doors of the pilothouse blew open.

The collier's five-inch deck gun was in a circular turret on the vessel's stern. The breech area is covered with a tarpaulin to protect against saltwater spray. Photo courtesy of Scott Jenkins.

The captain stayed on his feet only because he had been holding the hand-rail while looking out the pilothouse window. His first thought was, "Jesus, we've hit a mine." He then had to pry the hands of the panicked helmsman off the wheel. Next he went for the ship's papers.

The acoustic type torpedo, from the German submarine *U-853*, was designed to home in on the sounds of ships' screws and struck aft where the engines and steering apparatus were located. Several crewmen were killed immediately. Others were to die in the following minutes.

For protection against U-boats, the *Black Point* carried a five-inch gun aft manned by four U.S. Navy gunners. One of the gunners was killed during the explosion. Another was seriously injured when he was blown 45 feet into the air. Luckily he was blown forward away from the rapidly sinking stern section.

In the radioshack, the explosion had thrown the radioman to the deck. He picked himself up and instinctively banged out an SOS. To maintain a continuous beacon to mark the stricken vessel's position, the radioman placed a book on the telegraph key and then scrambled on deck. The distress signal was picked up by a nearby Yugoslav freighter and relayed to U.S. anti-submarine forces. Naval vessels would find the German U-boat responsible for the attack and sink her (see episode 6).

The *Black Point* was sinking fast and the order to abandon ship was given. While one lifeboat was lowered, a seaman became fouled in a line and was hanging upside down by one foot. A shipmate freed him by cutting the line. The quick thinking seaman then managed to loosen a jammed liferaft, probably saving the last 17 men to get off—including the captain.

Fifteen minutes after being struck by the torpedo, the collier rolled to her port side, capsized, and sank within sight of land. Twelve of the crew went to the bottom with her. Thirty-four survivors escaped in two lifeboats and one liferaft. The lifeboats were powered by what the *Black Point*'s captain called 'Armstrong engines'—oars. However, Coast Guard boats responding to the disaster towed them to shore.

The *Black Point* had been built as a freighter in 1918 at Camden, New Jersey; later she was converted into a collier. The ship now lies about three-and-one-half miles southeast of Point Judith Lighthouse. The wreck is in two sections. Her intact, upright stern section, blown off during the attack, is approximately 600 yards south of the bow section in about 85 feet of water. The stern's anemone-encrusted deck gun and turret was probably the most recognizable feature and a photographer's delight until the turret tipped over in 1987. The bow section is upside down in approximately 95 feet of water, buried to the waterline. Many hull plates have fallen off allowing easy penetration, and the wreck is wide open inside. The hull extends up 50 feet off the bottom. Visibility, often over 25 feet, is better than one might expect, considering the mud bottom. The wreck provides good lobstering.

The *Black Point*'s deck gun was of no use when the collier was torpedoed by the submerged U-boat. Photo by Bill Campbell.

The deck gun was the stern's most recognizable feature until 1987 when the anemone-encrusted turret tipped over. Photo by Bill Campbell.

A skull and other skeletal remains inside the wreck. Twelve of the collier's crew went to the bottom with her. Photo by Bill Campbell.

Ordnance is often recovered by divers. The five-inch shell and small arms ammunition shown here were retrieved by Frank Benoit. Photo by the author.

U. S. Naval Ammunition Depot, Hingham, Mass.
6 Pounder................Case Gun
Fixed Case Ammunition................1 Round

## 8. Torpedo Target—USS *L-8*

| | | |
|---|---|---|
| **Type of vessel** | : | submarine |
| **Surface tons** | : | 456 |
| **Length** | : | 167.4 feet |
| **Beam** | : | 14.8 feet |
| **Hull construction** | : | steel |
| **Location** | : | 3 miles south of Brenton Reef Light |
| **Lat. and long.** | : | 41-22.88 N, 71-22.14 W |
| **Approximate depth of water:** | | 110 feet |

At the beginning of the First World War, the L-class was the latest in the progression of United States submarines. Armament included a three-inch deck gun in addition to four bow torpedo tubes and eight torpedoes. The deck gun was the first to be installed on a United States submarine. It was inspired by the success of German U-boats early in the war, using deck guns to sink unarmed merchant ships, thus saving torpedoes, and extending the length of their war cruises. The new deck gun was housed in a watertight well beneath the deck and had to be raised before it could be fired.

The *L-8* (SS-*48*) was launched in April 1917, just 17 days after the United States declared war, as the first submarine off the ways at the Portsmouth (N.H.) Naval Shipyard, after which hundreds were to follow.

The *L-8* under construction, the first of hundreds to be built at the Portsmouth (N.H.) Naval Shipyard. Photo courtesy of the shipyard.

The submarine in drydock. Photo courtesy of the National Archives.

Although she was launched very early in the war, and her armament was formidable, the *L-8* never engaged in a war action; in fact no other American submarines played a major role in World War I. One L-class boat did manage to survive the unique experience of being straddled by two U-boats, having one fire a torpedo at her, miss, and sink the second U-boat.

For two years after the war, the *L-8* served with a flotilla assigned to China. By 1922, only five years after first launching, the L-class submarine was obsolete. The *L-8*, by then attached to the West Coast Submarine Flotilla at San Pedro, California, was ready for decommissioning. She left San Pedro under her own power on July 25 and arrived at Hampton Roads, Virginia on September 28. She was decommissioned there November 15, 1922. Two years later, she was laid up at the Philadelphia Navy Yard, waiting to be stripped before disposal.

During the war, 28 Allied capital ships, battleships and cruisers had been sunk by Germany's U-boats. That demonstration of vulnerability impelled world-wide naval designers to increase the armor plating of large warships to better protect them against torpedo attack. In turn, a search was launched for more destructive weaponry. In the United States, the Newport Naval Torpedo Station developed an exotic answer: a magnetic influence exploder that would sense disturbance of the Earth's magnetic field as a metal-hulled ship moved through the water. The exploder was designed to fire a charge in the warhead of a torpedo as it passed under an armor-plated ship's unprotected lower hull. The blast was calculated to break the back of even a massive battleship. By February 1924 the development was ready for live testing with a fully loaded warhead, but the Navy refused to provide a battleship for use as a target.

By January 1925 the compelling need to prove the worth of the development scaled down the request to a more modest target—an obsolete submarine hulk. After initially rejecting even that compromise, the Navy agreed to provide one of the four L-class submarines that were then being stripped at Philadelphia. Of the four, the *L-8* was found to be the most sea-worthy although she had to be towed to Newport for the test.

On May 26, 1926 the first of two torpedoes equipped with the new exploder was fired at the submarine; it passed harmlessly underneath, an ignored omen of how ineffectual the new device would prove to be. The second did explode in a vast column of gas and water that sent the *L-8* to the bottom.

The commander of the Newport Torpedo Station, Captain Thomas Hart, referred to the exploder test in a letter to the Chief of Ordnance as, "the opening of a new phase of torpedo warfare which gives the U.S. a tremendous advantage over any prospective enemy." Captain Hart's claim was anything but prophetic. It's irony was borne out during the first two years of World War II, when U.S. torpedoes equipped with the same magnetic influence exploders were totally ineffective against the Japanese. The torpedoes ran too deep, and their highly touted exploders fired either prematurely—or not at all. Those deficiencies were never revealed because the *L-8* was the only destructive test conducted during 19 years of pre-World War II magnetic exploder development.

The wreck site is well known. There is no appreciable current to add hazard to the 110-foot dive. However, visibility is almost always bad—usually five to ten feet; 15 feet is highly unusual.

Exploration of the wreck reveals the *L-8* listing 20 degrees to port. Considering that the submarine was sunk by a torpedo, the pressure hull is far more intact than one would expect. The exterior of the conning tower and other streamlining exteriors, however, are badly decomposed.

Several compartment hatches are open, inviting penetration of the submarine's interior. The forward torpedo room is accessible through the torpedo loading hatch and a very large damage hole. A diver entering through the damage hole is forward in the room and can swim aft over the torpedo tubes.

The interior is covered with two feet of sediment that is stirred up by even the most cautious diver—until the poor visibility deteriorates to zero, literally zero.

Above: a torpedo equipped with a magnetic influence exploder passing harmlessly under the *L-8* during tests off Newport, R.I. This torpedo did not explode and should have been an omen of how ineffectual the new device would prove to be. Below: on the second try the *L-8* was sunk. This was the only destructive test ever conducted during 19 years of pre-World War II magnetic exploder development. Photos courtesy of the Naval Historical Center.

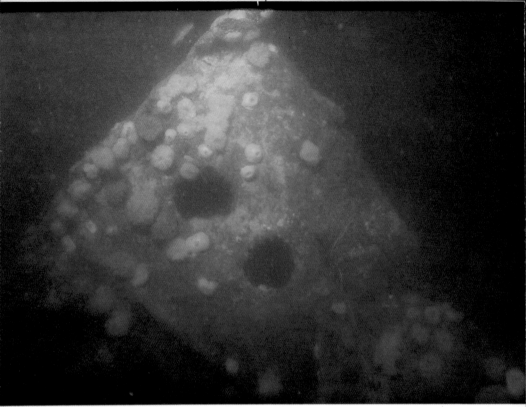

The conning tower's streamlined housing has separated from the pressure hull. Photo by Bill Campbell.

One of *L-8*'s two screws. The other was retrieved by divers. Photo by Brian Skerry.

In the foward torpedo room, looking aft over a brass torpedo tube. Photo by Bill Campbell.

Inside the forward torpedo room. Note the dangling electrical conduits and pipes. Photo by Brian Skerry.

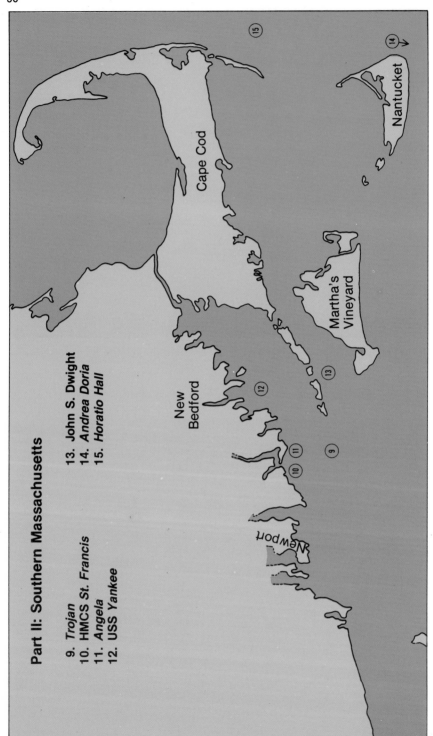

## Part II: Southern Massachusetts

9. *Trojan*
10. *HMCS St. Francis*
11. *Angela*
12. *USS Yankee*

13. *John S. Dwight*
14. *Andrea Doria*
15. *Horatio Hall*

# 9. Impenetrable Fog—*Trojan*

| | | |
|---|---|---|
| **Type of vessel** | : | freighter |
| **Gross tons** | : | 1,786 |
| **Length** | : | 261.5 feet |
| **Beam** | : | 38 feet |
| **Hull construction** | : | iron |
| **Location** | : | 4 miles WSW of Cuttyhunk |
| **Lat. and long.** | : | 41-22.33 N, 71-00.24 W |
| **Approximate depth of water:** | | 100 feet |

Before the Cape Cod Canal was completed in 1915, Vineyard Sound was the path coastal steamers used to and from Boston. A lightship was anchored at the western entrance to that heavily traveled waterway as a beacon for ships at night and in bad weather.

Seaman dreaded the area during periods of thick fog, particularly with ships converging there. On January 22, 1906, the 18-year-old freighter *Trojan* was feeling her way cautiously, groping through a dense fog with fog horn sounding and lookouts posted. The freighter's captain knew he was only a few miles from the Vineyard Lightship, but he could not see the familiar beacon.

The ship had been built at Wilmington, Delaware in 1888 as a collier for the Boston Towboat Company. She had been christened the *Orion* but when that company merged with the Boston and Philadelphia Steamship Company in 1905, the ship was renamed the *Trojan*. The new owners converted her to a general cargo freighter by installing a 'tweendecks.'

The *Trojan* was built in 1888. Photo courtesy of The Mariners' Museum, Newport News, Virginia.

The *Nacoochee* ramming the *Trojan*. Sketch by Chris Hugo.

Two-and-one-half months after the conversion, the *Trojan* left Philadelphia with a general cargo, bound for Boston. As the freighter neared the entrance to Vineyard Sound, her captain decided to anchor and continue the voyage only after the impenetrable fog lifted. The *Trojan* was almost stopped when the steel bow of the passenger liner *Nacoochee*, also bound for Boston, shot out of the thick fog and crashed into the freighter's port side. Those on board the *Trojan* said the liner was steaming at a fast clip "carrying a bone in her teeth."

The *Nacoochee* had struck just forward of amidships, cutting a huge hole that extended ten feet below the waterline. The liner's steel prow penetrated so deeply that the *Trojan* heeled to starboard until it was feared she would capsize. The freighter started to fill with water, then righted, freeing the *Nacoochee*. The *Trojan* was sinking so fast that her crew had no time to cut the lifeboats free. They scampered into the rigging as the ship settled by the bow. The *Nacoochee* stood by while her crew threw lines to the men trapped in the rigging. The entire crew of 27 were rescued, and fortunately there were no injuries.

Although the *Nacoochee* sustained only slight damage to her bow, her captain belatedly displayed caution; he anchored and waited 39 hours before the fog cleared before continuing his voyage.

The Steamboat Inspection Service, meeting in Providence, Rhode Island three months later, found the *Nacoochee*'s captain at fault. They determined that the liner was traveling too fast in the dense fog, the captain used poor judgement, and he did not display good seamanship. His license was suspended for 30 days. The *Trojan*'s captain was exonerated of all blame.

When the *Trojan* sank in about 100 feet of water, she carried a valuable cargo. It included bronze ingots and tin ingots, several tons of which were recovered by sport divers in 1972. This wreck produces many artifacts, especially small bottles from the 300 crates of bottles that were listed as part of the cargo.

The *Trojan* is lying on a muddy bottom, so the visibility is usually poor. The stern is somewhat intact, listing to the starboard side. The wooden decking is intact in some areas and completely disintegrated in others. Where there is no decking it is easy to penetrate the wreck between iron I beams. There is a large opening in the side of the hull and, with the generally poor visibility, an unwary diver can unknowingly swim into the interior.

Forward of the boiler, the wreck is flattened out and scattered. Fishing trawlers are allowed to drag in this area during the latter part of the summer. Their nets stir up the sediment, vastly reducing the already poor visibility. A large fishing net trapped on the wreck is a hazard in which a diver can become entangled.

A trawler's net on the wreck is not only a hazard to divers, but also to marine organisms, such as this shark. Photo by the author.

Bronze ingots, each weighing 25 pounds, recovered by sport divers in 1972. Photos from the author's collection.

# 10. Lend-Lease Four-Stacker—HMCS *St. Francis*

| | | |
|---|---|---|
| **Type of vessel** | : | destroyer |
| **Gross tons** | : | 1,060 |
| **Length** | : | 314.3 feet |
| **Beam** | : | 31.7 feet |
| **Hull construction** | : | steel |
| **Location** | : | 2 miles off Acoaxet, MA |
| **Lat. and long.** | : | 41-27.42 N, 71-06.20 W |
| **Approximate depth of water:** | | 60 feet |

German troops invaded Poland on the morning of September 1, 1939. Two days later, France and Britain declared war against Germany. World War II had been launched. Untold millions would die or be maimed, cities and historic treasures would be obliterated, and atrocities would lay bare the worst side of man's nature.

Many had predicted a second World War. One eminent military authority, Field Marshal Foch of France, had predicted not only a war but, further, "The next war will begin where the last one ended." Naval experts on both sides of the Atlantic agreed that submarine warfare and anti-submarine tactics would be a continuation of World War I, during which U-boats finally had been neutralized by the convoy system and depth charges. That knowledge inclined Britain to make light of the U-boat threat. Relatively low shipping losses in the early months of the war contributed to that complacency. With the fall of France on June 22, 1940, the entire strategic balance changed. Germany had gained ports to base her U-boats in occupied France, with an ocean front of 2,500 miles.

Both sides had entered the conflict unprepared: Germany with too few U-boats and Britain with only 180 destroyers. Germany held the advantage, however; the U-boat's increased operational area made the number of available escort vessels inadequate for the task of protecting Allied convoys. By 1940, Admiral Karl Doenitz, Commander-in-Chief, U-boats, was so heartened by the increased output of U-boats that he declared, "I will show that the U-boat alone can win this war."

President Franklin D. Roosevelt was aware of the crisis facing England. Although the United States was a neutral country, Roosevelt's interpretation of international neutrality laws was pro-British. Were Britain to fall, the United States might be the next object of German attack.

Shortly after the beginning of the war the United States was supplying arms and ammunition to England. Roosevelt initiated "cash-and-carry." Theoretically, any of the belligerents could procure military supplies from the United States—as long as they paid cash and carried those supplies in their own ships. This was fine with England; she ruled the seas. Germany, however, as had been intended, was unable to take advantage of the offer; her merchant fleet was blockaded by British warships. Roosevelt's "cash-and-carry" plan began to break down as England ran short of cash. He circumvented that problem with "lend-lease," lending war materials to England in exchange for leased bases in the Western Hemisphere.

During the summer of 1940, however, German U-boats were close to fulfilling Admiral Doenitz' claim that the U-boat alone could win the war. Britain needed convoy escorts to combat that threat. Although Roosevelt had already stretched the interpretation of international neutrality laws through "lend-lease," the United States supplied Britain with 50 old four-stacker destroyers. In return, the United States received 99-year leases for bases in the Bahamas, Jamaica, St. Lucia, Trinidad, Antigua, and British Guiana—bases that were crucial for protection of the Panama Canal.

Roosevelt did not consult Congress about his intentions because of anticipated isolationist opposition. The isolationists in Congress and throughout the country denounced the action as dictatorial and a violation of American neutrality that would certainly lead to war. Many, however, praised the action, showing they were ready to commit the nation to all-out aid to Britain.

Roosevelt had been able to circumvent Congress by arranging the deal through executive agreement instead of treaty. A debate would have lasted for months. Attorney General Jackson found two old laws and a decision of the Supreme Court to uphold the presidential right "to dispose of vessels of the Navy and unneeded naval materials." Also, according to the Attorney General, the transference of the over-age destroyers would be within neutrality limitations because they had not been built specifically for a belligerent nation. Most of the destroyers had been built more than 20 years earlier during World War I to combat a similar U-boat threat.

They may have been obsolete, but Britain desperately needed escort vessels to protect the convoys carrying "lend-lease" war material. British

The USS *Bancroft* (DD-*256*) was one of the "lend-lease" destroyers assigned to the Royal Canadian Navy. She was renamed the *St. Francis*. Photo courtesy of the Naval Historical Center.

Admiral of the Fleet, Sir James Somerville, wrote in his memoirs, "Had there been no American four-stacker destroyers available, and, had they not gone into service escorting trade convoys when they did, the outcome of the struggle against the U-boat and the subsequent outcome of the European War itself, might have been vastly different."

The USS *Bancroft* (DD-*256*) was launched on March 21, 1919, several months after signing of the armistice ending the military phase of World War I. The four-stacker destroyer was part of the Atlantic Fleet until she was placed in reserve in November of the same year. Three years later the *Bancroft* was decommissioned and remained in mothballs until the threat of war restored her to activity. She was recommissioned in December 1939 and again joined the Atlantic Fleet.

On September 24, 1940, the *Bancroft* was again decommissioned from U.S. Navy service. This time, however, she was transferred to Great Britain at Halifax, Nova Scotia as one of the 50 "lend-lease" destroyers. She was assigned to the Royal Canadian Navy and renamed HMCS *St. Francis*.

Once in the hands of the Royal Canadian Navy, several alterations were made on the old destroyer. Asdic, the anti-submarine sounding system that the United States Navy called sonar (*so*und *na*vigation *r*anging), was installed. One boiler was sacrificed to increase fuel capacities. The two four-inch deck guns were replaced with anti-aircraft weapons, and the 12 torpedo tubes were removed in favor of "k" and "y" guns—depth charge projectors. Also, the bridge and pilot house were enclosed, improving crew conditons for the cold North Atlantic.

After refitting, the *St. Francis* spent the remainder of the year based at Halifax; in November she searched for the German pocket battleship *Admiral Scheer* following her attack on convoy Hx.84. From January 1941, the destroyer served as one of the much-needed escorts for the North Atlantic convoys and made several attacks upon U-boats.

As newer, faster and more modern vessels were commissioned, they replaced the old four-stackers as convoy escorts. The *St. Francis* was converted into a net tender for training exercises at Annapolis Basin, Nova Scotia in February 1944.

On June 11, 1945 the *St. Francis* was decommissioned for the final time, her armament removed, and sold for scrap. While under tow en route to Baltimore, Maryland she sank about two miles off Acoaxet, Massachusetts on July 14, 1945. The destroyer was rammed by the collier *Windind Gulf* in a dense fog. There was no loss of life or injuries, although a large hole was stove in the hull of the *St. Francis*.

A thick film of oil from the wreck blanketed a two-mile stretch of Horseneck Beach in Westport, Massachusetts. A 16-foot lifeboat, two life rafts, and several sailors' sea bags were found on the oil-soaked beach.

The wreck is often mistakenly called the *St. Clair* (USS *Williams*). This four-stacker was decommissioned in August 1944. She remained in Halifax as a firefighting and damage control training hulk in Bedford

Wreckage is scattered in 60 feet of water. Photo by Bill Kurz.

Basin. The *St. Clair* was turned over to the Canadian War Assets Corporation late in 1946. The corporation sold the vessel to a Mr. Simon of Halifax. The *St. Clair*, however, was still in Halifax as late as 1950.

The *St. Francis* sank in only 60 feet of water and was declared a menace to navigation. The owner of the wreck, Boston Metals Company of Baltimore, wrote the Army Corps of Engineers, "This company is the sole owner of this vessel and here-by abandon the wreck to the United States, and disclaims any further responsibility in the matter."

The *St. Francis* was blasted with dynamite, and portions of her wreckage were removed by salvagers. Thirty feet of the bow is intact, sitting upright, pointing toward shore. The rest of the wreck, large plates scattered over the bottom with occasional sandy gaps between them, extends perpendicular to the shore. A stack of tubes is all that remains of the boiler. Visibility ranges from poor to excellent, and on a good day the *St. Francis* is a very pretty dive.

A piece of hull plate containing a porthole. Photo by Mike Casalino.

A British kerosene lamp recovered from the destroyer by Bill Carter. Photo by the author.

## 11. Unexpected Find—*Angela*

| | | |
|---|---|---|
| **Type of vessel** | : | cement barge |
| **Gross tons** | : | 8,512 |
| **Length** | : | 420 feet |
| **Beam** | : | 80 feet |
| **Hull construction** | : | galvanized steel |
| **Location** | : | off Horseneck Beach, Westport, MA |
| **Lat. and long.** | : | 41-27.40 N, 71-02.20 W |
| **Approximate depth of water:** | | surface to 30 feet |

During 1962–63 the Atlantic Cement Company of Ravena, New York, spent $9.6 million to have three barges built at the Avondale Shipyard in New Orleans, Louisiana. When finished the *Angela*, *Adelaide* and *Alexander* were the largest ocean-going cement barges in the world. They were unique because they were unmanned and self-unloading. Each barge contained two giant screw augers extending almost three-quarters of the vessels length. They mixed the dry cement with air and carried it forward to be blown out into silos on shore.

Near the end of April 1971, the *Angela* loaded 90,000 barrels of cement at Ravena. She was then taken in tow for the long journey down the Hudson River. The tug was from the Moran Towing Company of Greenwich, Connecticut, Atlantic Cement's exclusive tower. The barge unloaded 26,000 barrels of cement in Bayonne, New Jersey before the tug, with the *Angela* in tow, headed for Boston via the Cape Cod Canal. On March 3 the seas began to pick up in Rhode Island Sound, making it difficult for the tug to control the barge. Meanwhile, a heavy fog set in. The tug's towing cable parted, and the captain decided to anchor his tow until the seas calmed and his crew could set a new cable. He dropped the *Angela*'s anchor by remote control, dialing his telephone. The signal activated the barge's anchor release. Two men were put aboard to adjust the scope of the anchor line. When that was completed, they were taken off and the tug headed for port to wait out the storm.

The tug's captain had unintentionally left his tow in a precarious position. In the dense fog the *Angela* had been anchored close to Hen and Chickens Reef off Horseneck Beach, Westport, Massachusetts. When the tug returned to pick up her tow, the barge was impaled on Old Cock Rock, a pinnacle of rock extending up from the reef. Either the *Angela*'s anchor had dragged or the cyclonic storm had swung her around onto the reef.

Waves were washing over the barge's deck and the tug's crew could do nothing but check twice each day to see if the *Angela*'s position had changed. The weather kept them off the wreck for two days. When divers inspected the hull they found extensive damage. The barge was declared a total loss and the diesel fuel was removed to prevent pollution. The two large diesel engines that operated the screw augers were recovered and sold to a power plant. Scuba divers did not immediately dive the wreck

Above: the *Angela* impaled on Old Cock Rock in 1971. Photo courtesy of Bill Carter. Below: storms have taken their toll from the cement barge and salvors have burned off pieces of the galvanized steel hull, but the exposed wreck is still easy to find. Photo by the author.

because the *Angela*, being a barge, was not expected to have many exciting artifacts.

Several months after the grounding, a group of divers, including Bill Carter, was searching for a wreck in the vicinity and decided to eat lunch on the *Angela*. During the meal they noticed the water was clear and inviting. They had not found the wreck they had been searching for, so they dove the barge. The divers retrieved several bronze lanterns, the owner's plaque and many other artifacts. However, the best find would come when they later revisited the wreck. On that dive they discovered a 300-foot tunnel walkway, three decks down and beneath the cargo holds. The tunnel contained 54 brass portholes that were used as inspection ports and for access to the screw augers that carried the cement. The portholes, on shelves on either side of the walkway, were removed by the divers. They are identical to the portholes on the *Queen Mary*. Thousands of the same type of porthole were ordered by the British Government during the Depression as a means to keep shipyard workers employed. This program was similar to the Works Progress Administration (WPA) in the United States.

The *Angela*'s portholes had originally been installed in the British Victory ships *Liberty* and *Belmont*. Victory ships made their appearance later in World War II, and were larger and faster than Liberty ships (see episode 25). After World War II the two ships were sold for scrap to Boston Metals. The portholes were salvaged and sold to Avondale Shipyard where they were installed in the *Angela* as inspection ports.

The exposed wreck sits on Hen and Chickens Reef and is easy to find. The hull is broken open and the decks have collapsed in several places, allowing easy access to the interior. If entry is made on the starboard side, the water is calm and the diver is usually protected from the surge. Marine growth covers most of the wreck, making it an excellent dive for macro photography.

All the portholes have been removed and the tunnel and other compartments are dark and dangerous. A diver should not penetrate without a line and then should be extremely cautious.

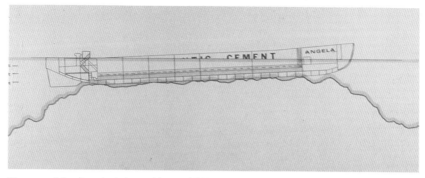

Diagram of the *Angela* sitting on Hen and Chickens Reef. The tunnel walkway where the portholes were found is highlighted in yellow. Diagram courtesy of Bill Carter.

Inside the *Adelaide*'s (a sisterbarge) tunnel. The portholes, installed to allow inspection of the screw augers, lie vertically on shelves on both sides of the walkway. Photo by Paul Sherman.

A porthole before recovery by a diver. Photo by Paul Sherman.

Bill Carter and Paul Kelly with 8 of the 54 portholes recovered from the tunnel. Photo by Paul Sherman.

# 12. Converted Liner—USS *Yankee*

| | | |
|---|---|---|
| **Type of vessel** | : | warship |
| **Gross tons** | : | 6,888 |
| **Length** | : | 406.1 feet |
| **Beam** | : | 48.4 feet |
| **Hull construction** | : | iron |
| **Location** | : | 5 miles S of New Bedford, MA |
| **Lat. and long.** | : | 41-32.45 N, 70-52.45 W |
| **Approximate depth of water:** | | 55 feet |

The closing years of the nineteenth century were a turning point in American history. They marked the end of an era of relative isolation and the beginning of a period during which the United States would emerge as a world power. The end of the Spanish-American War is generally accepted as the dividing line between the two epochs.

During the 1890's, many newspaper editors pounded the drum of Manifest Destiny. Captain Alfred Mahan, a prominent naval officer and writer, was one of the foremost proponents of expansion. He was a firm believer in a canal linking the Atlantic and Pacific Oceans, under complete American control. For geographic reasons, it would have to be in Central America and the United States would need Caribbean bases to protect it.

Another vocal expansionist was the young Henry Cabot Lodge of Massachusetts. He felt that Cuba should be taken by force from Spain, and the islands of the Pacific "snatched from the grasping hands of European nations." There were, however, vigorous opponents to expansion, President Grover Cleveland for one. Many New Englanders were strong in their denunciation of what they termed imperialism.

Captain Mahan believed America's best offense and defense was a strong navy. The stronger navy demanded by Mahan and other expansionists began to materialize during the 1890's.

The advocates of expansion needed a cause and found one in the Cuban insurrection of 1895. Spanish measures of repression were harsh and the atrocity stories, exaggerated in the columns of the "yellow" press, horrified America. Public opinion demanded that the Spanish cease hostilities.

On February 15, 1898 a tragic explosion destroyed the *Maine* in Havana Harbor. The loss of the U.S. battleship and 266 men was the breaking point. In April Congress passed four resolutions that amounted to a declaration of war. Although the navy had increased in size and efficiency since 1890, more ships were quickly needed. The conflict would not be restricted to Cuba. It would also include Spain's Pacific possessions. On paper, the naval strength of Spain was greater than that of the United States: 137 warships to 86. However, those figures were deceptive. American warships were newer and better armed.

The passenger liner *El Norte* was built in 1892 by the Newport News Shipbuilding and Drydock Company of Newport News, Virginia for the

The auxiliary cruiser *Yankee* participated in the Spanish-American War. Four of her five-inch guns are visible in hull ports. Photo courtesy of the Naval Historical Center.

The *Yankee* on May 2, 1898 at the New York Navy Yard. Four of her ten 5-inch guns are visible in hull ports and another is on the Forecastle. Photo courtesy of the Naval Historical Center.

Southern Pacific Company. She was bought by the Navy Department on April 6, 1898 and renamed the *Yankee*.

The liner was well-suited for conversion into an auxiliary cruiser. She could make 16 knots, fast for her time. More important, the ship was large enough to take heavy armament. The *Yankee*'s hull was pierced for eight broadside hull casemates, each containing a 5-inch rapid-fire gun. Also, she was armed with two additional 5-inch guns, six 6-pounders and two Colt Automatics. Accommodations were retained for a wartime crew of 15 officers and 267 men. The conversion from liner to cruiser was accomplished at the New York Navy Yard, with most of her crew reservists from the New York Naval Militia. Many had trained on the old ship-of-the-line *New Hampshire* (see episode 22).

The *Yankee* was commissioned on April 14, 1898 and the following month left New York to patrol between Cape Cod and Cape Henlopen in search of Spanish merchant ships. On May 29 the auxiliary cruiser was ordered to Cuba and arrived off Santiago on June 3. The *Yankee* participated in a night action with Spanish torpedo boats the following night.

On June 6 the cruiser participated in the bombardment of Spanish fortifications at Santiago. The American fleet fired about 2,000 rounds. The Spanish batteries at Morro Castle and Fort Aguadores were hit frequently, with the loss of three men killed and 40 wounded. Their reply was feeble; the *Massachusetts* was hit once, but the *Yankee* and other warships were unscathed. The following day, she and another warship engaged two Spanish gunboats at Guantanamo, driving them into the upper bay. On June 10, under a heavy protecting fire, the *Yankee* and two other warships landed a force of 600 marines at Guantanamo Bay. The marines were the first organized United States force to land in Cuba, and after fierce fighting they captured the important port. Three days later, while patrolling off Cienfuegos, the *Yankee* had another encounter with two Spanish gunboats. Again, her heavy fire forced them to withdraw into the harbor.

The cruiser continued blockade duty until her dwindling supply of coal forced her to head for Key West. En route the *Yankee* stopped at the Isle of Pines where she destroyed five Spanish fishing vessels.

The cruiser was ordered from Key West to New York and Norfolk to take on ammunition for the blockading fleet. She returned to Guantanamo in late July for the tedious and dangerous job of transferring her cargo of ammunition to various warships.

Spain sued for peace the following month, and the *Yankee* returned to New York. She was decommissioned at the Philadelphia Navy Yard on March 16, 1899.

The "splendid little war," as Secretary of State John Hay termed it, netted the United States possession of Puerto Rico, Guam, and the Philippines, and a guardianship over Cuba.

The *Yankee* was recommissioned as a training ship in May 1903. In December 1904 she was ordered to make a round-trip to Panama to exchange marine garrisons in the Canal Zone. For the next year and a half

The cruiser aground off Westport in 1908, above; submerged in Buzzards Bay, below. Photos courtesy of Bill Carter.

she played a role in the United States' "Gunboat Diplomacy" in the Caribbean, moving from island to island in support of American forces and citizens.

In August 1906 the *Yankee* returned to the United States. She participated in President Theodore Roosevelt's Naval Review held at Oyster Bay, New York in September. During the same month she was again placed out of commission, but two years later the cruiser was recommissioned for a familiar duty—training. On August 19, 1908 the *Yankee* embarked a class of Naval Academy midshipmen for exercises off Fishers Island, Boston, and New Bedford, Massachusetts. In Newport, on September 20, Rhode Island Naval Militia were added, increasing her complement to 600 officers and men. Three days later a dense fog, compounded by smoke from forest fires, contributed to the cruiser running aground on Spindle Rock off Westport, Massachusetts.

The ship had grounded at high tide; her bow was seven to eight feet out of the water, and it was necessary to lighten her before she could be refloated. Divers tried to plug the many punctures in the cruiser's hull and her guns were removed. She was pulled off on December 4 but, while being towed to New Bedford, she sank in Buzzards Bay, about five miles south of that port.

The *Yankee* sank in about 55 feet of water and was periodically salvaged until September 1920. Then, considered a hazard to navigation, the cruiser was blown apart. Wreckage is flattened out on either side of the hull over a considerable distance. The main part of the hull, however, is distinguishable and can be followed from bow to stern with reasonable visibility. Some sections of the wreck extend six to ten feet off the bottom. The bow and stern are distinguishable only by the parts, the anchor hawser opening and the rudder posts. The wreck is loaded with portholes (she had about 180) and other artifacts typical of a navy vessel of that era. Solid brass railroad wheels, used on gun turrets to pivot the guns, can occasionally be found.

There can be moderate to strong currents in the area. Visibility is usually bad, one to five feet. On rare occasions, however, it can be as good as 20 feet. With the bad visibility, jagged pieces of metal wreckage are a hazard to divers.

Side scan sonar printout of the *Yankee*. Courtesy of Historical Maritime Group of New England.

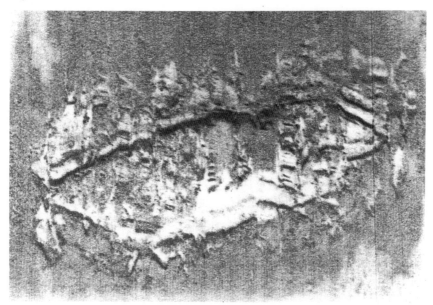

Pieces of steel wreckage
make an ideal site for sea
anemones to attach. Photo
by Bill Kurz.

Moments after the author took the photo, Chris Dillon found a dinner plate in this opening in
the wreckage.

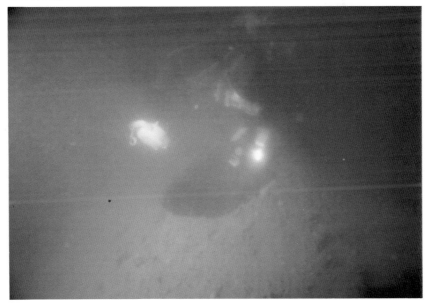

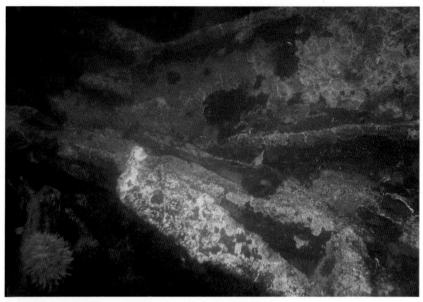

Wreckage is flattened out on both sides of the hull. Photo courtesy of Bill Carter.

An assortment of artifacts recovered from the *Yankee* by Bill Carter.

## 13. Rum Runner—*John S. Dwight*

| | | |
|---|---|---|
| **Type of vessel** | : | rum runner |
| **Gross tons** | : | 153 |
| **Length** | : | 112 feet |
| **Beam** | : | 27.3 feet |
| **Hull construction** | : | wood |
| **Location** | : | one mile off Nashawena Island |
| **Lat. and long.** | : | 41-23.26 N, 70-52.36 W |
| **Approximate depth of water:** | | 85 feet |

> Oh, we don't give a damn for our old Uncle Sam
> Way-o, whiskey and gin!
> Lend us a hand when we stand in to land
> Just give us time to run the rum in.
> —"The Smugglers' Chantey"
> Joseph Chase Allen, 1921

The mystery surrounding the scuttling of the rum runner *John S. Dwight* during Prohibition has never been solved. Whatever occurred on that day of April 6, 1923 was shrouded in fog at the time and in rumor ever since.

Records in Newport, Rhode Island, from where the *Dwight* set forth on her last voyage, show that her two captains had given fictitious names to the authorities. At least eight others were on board.

The *Dwight*, a steam schooner, left Newport, steamed out into Buzzards Bay and anchored. The captain of the mailboat from New Bedford to Cuttyhunk thought the vessel was in distress and spoke with one her captains. Several men, sunning on deck, hurried below, and the mailboat captain was told that the *Dwight* was having engine trouble, but the problem would soon be solved. When the mailboat returned to New Bedford her captain reported his suspicion that the *Dwight* was a rum runner.

Prohibition was four years old and bootleg booze was big business. The Eastern Seaboard was known as "Rum Row," where hootch-laden ships from Canada would anchor just beyond U.S. territorial waters. Under the cover of darkness, small vessels from American ports would load this illegal cargo and run it into some secluded shore. Many considered rum running an almost respectable form of protest against the unpopular Eighteenth Amendment (Prohibition).

The *Dwight* had been built as a collier in 1896 at Tomkins Cove, New York by Rodermund and Company. Two years later the steamer was purchased by the U.S. Navy and renamed the *Pawnee*. The collier served as a tug and salvage vessel at the New York Navy Yard until July 25, 1922 when she was sold to Seabury and DeZafro, Incorporated of New York. When she left Newport it was ostensibly to pick up a cargo of coal in Brooklyn, N.Y. The mailboat that chanced upon her, however, found her well east of her proposed course. The *Dwight* was waiting for night to cover her rum running.

The *Dwight*'s two captains, Malcolm Carmichael of Jersey City, N.J. and John King of Brooklyn, could not have asked for better conditions to evade the U.S. Coast Guard. A heavy fog set in that night.

Carrying a cargo of beer and ale, the *Dwight* used the cover of dense fog to reach the entrance of Vineyard Sound about 6 a.m. What then happened is speculation and rumor. Some report machine-gun fire; others claim that an explosion occurred. About the same time, the men at the Gay Head Coast Guard Station heard a long whistle from the Sound. Thinking it to be a distress signal, they launched a boat, but the engine failed and the crew was forced to row.

Shortly after 7 a.m. the fog lifted, and a lookout at the Cuttyhunk Coast Guard Station spotted the *Dwight* flying a distress signal and sinking by the stern. They also launched a boat, but a strong current prevented them from getting through Canapitsit Channel, the normal route. They were forced to take the long route around the island.

When the Coast Guard boats finally reached the site, the *Dwight* had already sunk from view, but barrels of bottled ale labeled "Frontenac

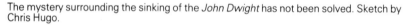

The mystery surrounding the sinking of the *John Dwight* has not been solved. Sketch by Chris Hugo.

Imported Stock Ale, Montreal" were bobbing on the surface. Nothing could be found of her crew. Twenty-four hours later, however, the results unfolded. Seven bodies wearing life preservers were found floating in Vineyard Sound, their faces badly battered. Some reports state their faces and fingertips were disfigured with acid, making identification impossible. Also, a small lifeboat drifted ashore on Martha's Vineyard, carrying only the body of Harry King, the son of one of the *Dwight*'s two captains. The back of his skull had been crushed by a blunt instrument. Lying beside the body was a small knife. The medical examiner of Edgartown, Martha's Vineyard made this profound announcement to the *Boston Evening Globe*: "In my opinion, there appears to have been a fight." The bodies of the two captains and the other crewmen were never found.

The morning of the incident, the pilot of a ship bound for Boston through Vineyard Sound saw the *Dwight* with davits for two lifeboats swinging empty and a boat with three men in it making for deserted Naushon Island. If there were survivors, they never came forward. The *Dwight*'s quarterboards, with her name painted in white on a black background, were found on Naushon Island, showing an attempt to conceal the steam schooner's identity.

Many rumors circulated regarding what happened on the Sound that morning. The crew and captains supposedly put up about $100,000 to buy booze, expecting to share the profits. The actual cargo of beer and ale had cost only about $4,000. Had the captains deceived the crew? Did they then plan to murder those not part of the plot? Was there a mutiny by part of the crew? Could the mutineers have been dissatisfied with their cut and wanted the remaining $96,000? Would Captain King murder his own son? Was his son in the plot and killed in the fight? Was Captain King murdered, and his body never recovered? A seaman later said he saw Carmichael, the other captain, in Havana ten days after the incident.

One rumor suggests that bootleggers, disguised as Coast Guardsmen, hijacked the *Dwight* in the dense fog, which might explain the reported machine-gun fire and explosion.

Investigation by State and Federal authorities produced an incredible amount of conflicting testimony. Seven weeks after the investigation began, the Massachusetts Attorney General announced the sinking was "as much a mystery as ever."

The incident, labeled by the *Boston Globe* "the bloodiest maritime mystery in New England history," will probably never be solved, but to fishermen from Woods Hole, the Vineyard, and New Bedford it provided an unexpected windfall. They gathered in many barrels of booze. The Coast Guardsmen from Gay Head brought back 11 barrels, but when one mysteriously disappeared the captain ordered the remaining ten tossed from the Gay Head cliffs.

The following summer Navy divers found the *Dwight*'s sea-cocks open: the steam schooner had been scuttled. Later, the Navy dropped four depth charges on the *Dwight* hoping to destroy her cargo. The flattened wreckage is in about 85 feet of water about one mile off Nashawena Island, one of the Elizabeth group that stretches seaward southwest of Cape Cod.

Whoever scuttled the *Dwight* did not want her or her cargo to be found, but the wreck is now a popular dive site. Visibility is usually poor, averaging about 15 feet, and there are occasionally currents to contend with. The current, however, if not strong, can prove to be an advantage when a diver is digging in the sand and silt between wooden planks and beams, looking for beer and ale bottles. As the sediment is disturbed, the current will carry it away.

Barrel staves and many bottles are still scattered through the wreckage. Some bottles are green glass; others are brown. Most have no markings; others have raised letters identifying brewers including Tonawanda Brewing Co. of Tonawanda, N.Y., Indianapolis Brewing Co., and Bunker Hill Brewing Co.

The *Dwight*'s bell was recovered by a diver years ago.

Beer bottles are scattered through the wreckage. Photo by the author.

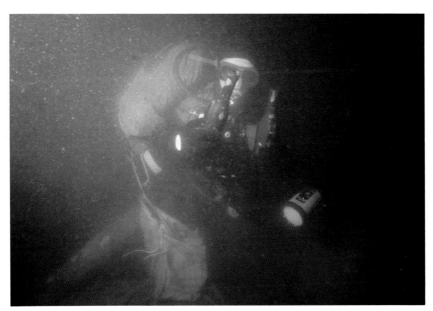

Chip Cooper holds up two beer bottles for the author to photograph.

Frank Benoit on the left, Chip Copper in the middle, and the author with beer bottles recovered from the rum runner. Photo by Roger Murphy.

## 14. Unlikely Disaster—*Andrea Doria*

| | | |
|---|---|---|
| **Type of vessel** | : | passenger liner |
| **Gross tons** | : | 29,082 |
| **Length** | : | 697.1 feet |
| **Beam** | : | 89.8 feet |
| **Hull construction** | : | steel |
| **Location** | : | 50 miles S of Nantucket Island, MA |
| **Lat. and long.** | : | 40–29.4 N, 69–50.5 W |
| **Approximate depth of water:** | | 240 feet |

The *Andrea Doria*, pride of Italy's fleet of passenger liners, was not the largest ship in the world, and she fell far short of being the fastest. However, there was no denying that she was the most beautiful ocean liner in existence during her short reign from 1951 to 1956.

The *Queen Elizabeth* and 12 other passenger ships exceeded the *Doria*'s 697-foot length and her trans-Atlantic crossings were slow compared to the three-and-one-half days' crossing time of the *United States*. However, in beauty of form and appointments the Italian vessel enjoyed unparalleled supremacy. Her silhouette and sleek lines created the illusion of motion even while the vessel was at anchor. However, her claim to beauty was more than just skin deep. Her interior was a glorious reflection of Renaissance Italy. Original oil paintings, tapestries, lifelike statuary, walls of murals and frescoes, pillars, and costly furnishings completed the illusion of a seaborne museum, reflecting the glories of Italy's artistic past.

The *Andrea Doria* was considered by many to be the most beautiful passenger liner of her day. Photo courtesy of the National Archives.

The murals in the First Class Lounge were a reflection of Renaissance Italy. Photo courtesy of Tom Roach.

Jon Hulburt found this piece of ceramic decoration within the wreck and brought it out onto the hull to photograph it.

The *Doria* was designed with passenger safety high on the list of priorities. Sixteen lifeboats provided capacity for 2,000 passengers and crew, far more than necessary for the 1,706 on board for her last voyage. Also, the most advanced safety measures available were incorporated into the vessel. Two radar screens to pierce the dense fog that always threatened a North Atlantic crossing, Loran for determining position at sea, radio direction finder, and a complete meterological station provided the finest navigational system available. Eleven watertight compartments extended two decks above the waterline to assure flotation even if two adjacent compartments were flooded, as long as the vessel did not list more than 20 degrees to either side. Such a list would open the tops of the compartments to seawater, an event unlikely to happen.

The beautiful vessel was painstakingly protected against disaster, fully equipped to accommodate survivors, and was under the command of an experienced, dedicated master whose sole responsibility for three and one-half years was to sail the *Doria* safely across the Atlantic. Captain Piero Calamai was ready to take an unblemished record with him to command of the newer Italian liner, *Christoforo Colombo*, after completing the 101st and 102nd crossings of the *Doria* which began at Naples on July 18, 1956. A strange combination of circumstances was to decree that the beautiful *Doria* would never return and Captain Calamai would be denied command of the *Colombo*.

The Swedish liner *Stockholm*, carrying 750 passengers and crew, steamed out of New York Harbor about 11:30 a.m. on Wednesday, July 25, bound for Copenhagen. Her course and the course of the *Doria* were to converge 50 miles south of Nantucket Island in an area known as the "Times Square of the Atlantic" because it handled so much of the North Atlantic shipping traffic, both east and west. The 1948 "International Convention for the Safety of Life at Sea" had established an eastbound course 20 miles south of the Nantucket Lightship. However, the course was voluntary and the Swedish Line was not a party to the convention. The master of the *Stockholm* had made 423 Atlantic crossings, all in as direct a routing as possible, without the 20-mile detour that would increase operating costs and jeopardize his record of on-time performance. His course on July 25 was one mile south of the Lightship. And so, in accordance with the Convention's recommendations, was the westbound Italian liner.

Fog engulfed the *Doria* as she churned toward New York. In token acknowledgement of the weather, Captain Calamai ordered her speed reduced from 23 to 21 1/2 knots. He was fully convinced that his ship's radar would provide adequate warning of approaching danger to permit evasive corrections of direction or speed.

Aboard the *Stockholm*, the bridge was under control of a young Third Officer, Johan Ernst Bogislaus Carstens Johannsen—Carstens to his shipmates. He had joined the ten-year-old vessel only two months earlier. Later testimony revealed that Carstens had his hands full with a helmsman who was known to let his mind wander from his task and permit the vessel to yaw off course a few degrees in either direction. Even that should have posed no problem, given the protection of radar.

As the two vessels came within radar range, each picked up the presence and location of the other. Technology had served its purpose, and disaster should have been averted. But, by almost unbelievable coincidence, the radar blips were misinterpreted by both ships and evasive maneuvering brought them into a collision course until they were within visual range. Then, in a decision that was to cost him his ship and his career, Captain Calamai ordered hard aport in a desperate effort to escape collision, relying on his vessel's high speed to take him out of the path of the *Stockholm*. All that he accomplished was to present starboard instead of bow to the onrushing Swedish liner. In doing so, he violated a basic safety rule: a vessel should turn toward oncoming danger to present a smaller target and minimize impact.

The *Stockholm*'s reinforced bow was designed to plow through the ice of Scandinavian waters. With a momentum built of 12,666 tons at 18 knots, she sheared into the *Doria*'s starboard side, aft of the bridge. Then, as her engines reversed, the Swedish vessel backed off, pulling out of the rupture and allowing the sea to rush in.

Nearing the end of her crossing, the *Doria*'s fuel was low. Empty tanks might have been filled with seawater for ballast but they were not. That left her riding high in the water, unstable, almost top-heavy, and easy prey for

The *stockholm*'s reinforced bow cuts into the *Doria*'s starboard side. Painting by Carl Evers; photo courtesy of the U.S. Navy Institute.

Her reinforced bow crushed during the collision, the *Stockholm* drifts as injured survivors are evacuated by a Coast Guard helicopter. Photo courtesy of the National Archives.

the type of damage inflicted on her. She listed rapidly and as the list approached 20 degrees, seawater flowed over her A Deck and down into the watertight compartments that were intended to ensure her survival. At this point, it was only a matter of how long it would take for the beautiful Italian liner to sink.

The critically damaged *Doria* remained afloat for 11 hours, while an armada of rescue vessels responded to her calls for aid. The *Stockholm* and five other vessels, including the *Ile de France*, rescued 1660 of her passengers and crew. The 46 who did not survive were lost as a result of the crash impact or panic. Five crewmen in the *Stockholm*'s forward crew quarters died instantly or later from injuries. Fifty-one people had died as a result of the collision.

Four months of hearings established that both vessels shared responsibility for the collision. The *Stockholm* was far north of the recommended route for eastbound vessels, her master was not on the bridge at the time, and she turned directly into the *Doria*. The Italian liner was speeding in fog, riding high with empty fuel tanks, and turned to port moments before impact. In actuality, if radar readings had been plotted to establish the course of each oncoming vessel, the converging paths would have been evident to the officers of both liners in adequate time to avoid collision.

The *Doria* lies 240 feet beneath the Altantic, 50 miles south of Nantucket Island. Strong ocean currents and the depth have discouraged all except the most adventurous divers from visiting the wreck, despite the attraction of her costly appointments and persistent rumors of abandoned valuables.

Peter Gimbel, a film maker, dove through a stream of bubbles rising from the wreckage the day after the sinking to take photographs for "Life" magazine. He has returned several times for filming and to cut through the hull to recover the safe of the Bank of Rome. That salvage was accomplished with the benefit of hot water suits, an underwater saturation station and a surface-supplied tri-mix breathing medium. All contributed to comfort, safety and dives of four to six hours.

There is another breed of divers, small in number but large in daring, who respond to the siren call of this underwater beauty. Sport divers in dry suits, hump-backed with air tanks and limited to 20-minute dives, have found their way to the *Doria*.

The liner's hull can be entered through an opening cut into the Foyer Deck during 1981 by Peter Gimbel's crew. The opening, 170 feet below the surface, provides access at 205 feet to a corridor that leads to the First Class Dining Room.

Entering the Dining Room is a disorienting experience because the tables are still secured to the flooring of the deck. With the ship on her side, however, the deck becomes a bulkhead, from which the tables protrude horizontally. All loose objects have tumbled to the original starboard bulkhead or against a dining room partition over which divers probe for crystal and dinnerware, all bearing the Italian Line's insignia, "Italia."

The *Doria*'s list was so severe her portside lifeboats could not be lowered. Photo courtesy of the National Archives.

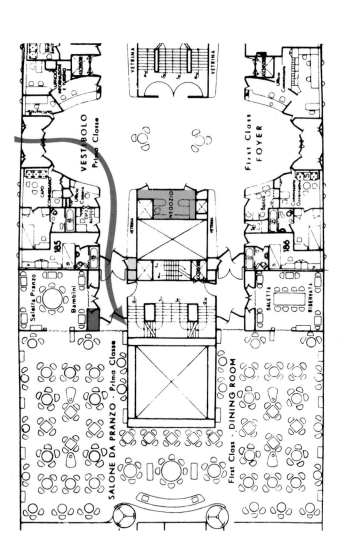

**VESTIBOLO** Primo Classe

First Class FOYER

185

186

Saletta Pranzo

Bambini

SALETTA

RISERVATA

VETRINA

VETRINA

NEGOZIO

VETRINA

VETRINA

**SALONE DA PRANZO - Prima Classe**

**First Class · DINING ROOM**

Diagram of the Foyer Deck. The red arrow illustrates the path divers follow, through the hull and into the corridor, to recover china and crystal. A china cabinet, also shown in red, collapsed and the contents fell onto the bulkhead below. A crystal cabinet is colored in yellow, the gift shop in blue.

The Foyer Deck's gift shop, about 15 feet directly beneath the corridor leading to the dining room, has produced many interesting artifacts. The famous art treasures that earned the liner her reputation for beauty, however, have probably been destroyed by exposure to saltwater. Those that have withstood the ravages of time and salinity are still to be recovered.

One important note of caution is that the wreck is extremely hazardous. The depth is beyond the normal range of everyday scuba divers, currents are very strong, and there is only one opening into and out of the Foyer Deck. The interior is in total darkness and clouds of silt rise when any surface is disturbed, making a dive light useless. Once the silt is disturbed, artifact discovery, retrieval and exit are performed in zero visibility. Another danger lies in the clusters of electrical cables that hang suspended like tentacles to entangle divers beyond the limits of their bottom time.

The dive is far from ended after divers complete their time on the wreck. Decompressing on the anchor line for about 45 minutes can be a harrowing experience. The strength of the current is so great at times that decompressing divers string out horizontally like flags, arms aching for relief.

Previous experience, physical condition, psychological state, and reaction to nitrogen narcosis determine whether or not the diver can endure a dive into eight atmospheres of pressure. Three divers have lost their lives on this wreck since 1981. However, divers continue to risk their lives to retrieve artifacts from the *Doria* because of the aura surrounding the wreck. To them, the artifacts are a priceless treasure, regardless of their intrinsic value.

Artifacts from the gift shop. Recovered and photographed by Steve Bielenda.

When sport divers first entered the corridor leading to the First Class Dining Room, they discovered a pile of china that had fallen from a cabinet on the other side of the corridor. Most of the china from this pile has been recovered and divers must now dig in the sediment to find pieces. Photo by Steve Gato.

Jon Hulburt proudly displays china as he swims out of the corridor. Photo by Chip Cooper.

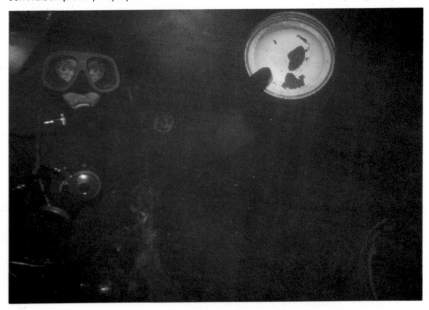

China bearing the Italian Line's insignia "Italia," recovered and photographed by the author.

A bathroom photographed by Bill Campbell.

A crystal cabinet containing hundreds of various types of stemware was emptied by divers. Photo by Jon Hulburt.

# 15. Perilous Pollock Rip Slue—*Horatio Hall*

| | | |
|---|---|---|
| **Type of vessel** | : | passenger liner |
| **Gross tons** | : | 3,168 |
| **Length** | : | 297 feet |
| **Hull construction** | : | steel |
| **Location** | : | Pollock Rip Shoals |
| **Approximate depth of water:** | | 35–40 feet |

Near the end of July 1892, William K. Vanderbilt and five guests were on his luxurious yacht *Alva* en route from Bar Harbor, Maine to Newport, Rhode Island. In a dense fog, the floating palace was approaching perilous Pollock Rip Slue, between Cape Cod's Monomoy Point and Nantucket Island. The yacht's captain decided to anchor and allow the fog to lift before steaming through the narrow channel. The next morning, still enveloped by fog, the 285-foot *Alva* was struck by the Metropolitan Line freighter *H.F. Dimock* and went to the bottom. Vanderbilt and his guests rushed to the lifeboats in their night clothes and were saved.

After several ships struck the submerged *Alva*, it was decided the wreck was a hazard to navigation and the wreck was blown apart with explosives. That was the fate of many shipwrecks and one of the reasons they resemble an underwater junkyard more than they do a ship.

The *Dimock*, with only slight damage to her bow, was quickly returned to the Boston-New York run, awaiting her next victim. Seventeen years later, that dubious distinction would be reserved for the passenger liner *Horatio Hall*, amazingly, near the same spot the *Dimock* had run down the *Alva*.

The *Horatio Hall* was named after the Maine Steamship Company's New York manager. Photo courtesy of The Mariners' Museum, Newport News, Virginia.

By the end of the Nineteenth Century, the Maine coast was increasing in popularity as a summer resort, so the Maine Steamship Company added two large, fast, steel-hulled steamers to their subsidiary, the Portland Line. One was the *Horatio Hall*, named for the line's New York manager. The passenger liner was built at Chester, Pennsylvania in 1898. The new steamer was put on the New York-to-Portland run.

Just before her loss, the *Hall*, along with the Portland Line, was bought by the Hartford & New York Transportation Company; however, she continued the New York-to-Portland run. Early in the morning of March 10, 1909, the *Hall* was steaming around Cape Cod bound for New York. In a heavy fog, she approached hazardous Pollock Rip Slue, near where the *Alva* had been sunk. Suddenly, the *Dimock*, bound for Boston, appeared out of the fog and rammed the liner broadside.

The freighter cut deep into the *Hall* and the ship was doomed. The *Dimock* kept her prow wedged into the liner's hull until passengers and part of the crew were transferred safely onto her bow. The *Hall*'s captain and some of his crew elected to stay on board.

This time the *Dimock* had suffered more damage than when she had rammed the *Alva*. Her captain was forced to beach the freighter on the sandy shore of Cape Cod, where all on board were rescued. The *Dimock* was eventually repaired and refloated.

The fatally stricken *Hall* drifted onto Pollock Rip Shoals and grounded. Her captain and the remaining crew were safely removed. Dur-

The *Hall* on Pollock Rip Shoals. Note the large hole by the stern mast made by the *Dimock* during the collision. Photo courtesy of The Mariners' Museum, Newport News, Virginia.

ing a subsequent storm, however, the liner was pulled into deeper water and was declared a menace to navigation like the *Alva* before her. The *Hall* was blown apart with explosives.

Like other passenger ships, the *Hall* carried cargo. Part of her general cargo was salvaged, and many homes in the Chatham area of Cape Cod display mirrors, china and silverware from the wreck.

The *Hall*, lying in 35 to 40 feet of water, still produces many artifacts, including portholes and china. The shifting sands in this area cover and uncover parts of the scattered wreckage. A good time to dive the wreck is after severe storms have cleared the sand from previously unexposed parts of the wreck.

A porthole complete with glass swingplate and storm cover. Photo by Brian Skerry.

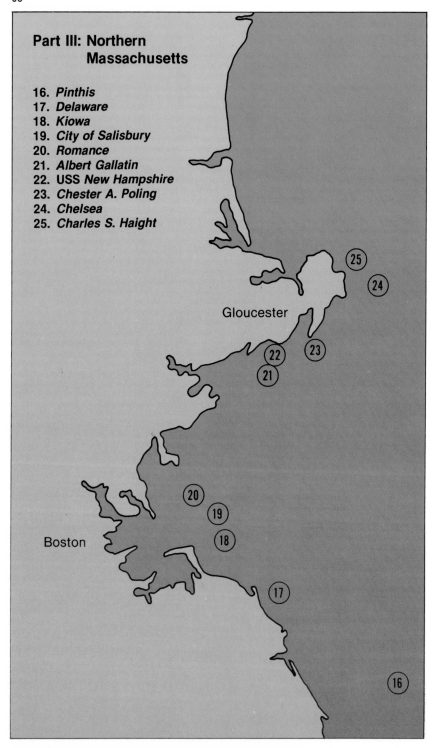

**Part III: Northern Massachusetts**

16. *Pinthis*
17. *Delaware*
18. *Kiowa*
19. *City of Salisbury*
20. *Romance*
21. *Albert Gallatin*
22. USS *New Hampshire*
23. *Chester A. Poling*
24. *Chelsea*
25. *Charles S. Haight*

Gloucester

Boston

# 16. Forty-Seven Lost in Flaming Inferno—*Pinthis*

| | | |
|---|---|---|
| **Type of vessel** | : | coastal tanker |
| **Gross tons** | : | 1,111 |
| **Length** | : | 206.8 feet |
| **Beam** | : | 35.6 feet |
| **Hull construction** | : | steel |
| **Location** | : | 6 miles East of Scituate, MA |
| **Lat. and long.** | : | 42–09.18 N, 70–33.48 W |
| **Approximate depth of water:** | | 100 feet |

The small coastal tanker *Pinthis*, built at Newburg, New York in 1919, had taken on 11,500 barrels of oil and gasoline at Fall River, Massachusetts, intending to discharge the cargo in Portland, Maine, and Chelsea, Massachusetts. The tanker was owned by Lake Tankers and leased to Shell Oil Company.

In a light cloak of fog the *Pinthis* had an uneventful passage through Cape Cod Canal and Cape Cod Bay, but as she was entering Massachusetts Bay the fog was thickening fast. Dense fog was usual in those waters, so her captain may not have been concerned. As dusk settled and the fog increased, he ordered the fog signal sounded: one blast with the tanker's whistle every minute.

The *Pinthis*' captain was unaware of the fast approach of the Merchants and Miners passenger liner *Fairfax*. The passenger ship had left Boston at 5 p.m. on June 10, 1930, heading south with 76 passengers and a crew of 80. Just after 7 p.m., although in a heavy fog, she was steaming at

The small coastal tanker *Pinthis* was not a pretty ship. Photo courtesy of Bill Carter.

11.2 knots. Suddenly, a ship appeared off the starboard bow, and simultaneously the liner's officers heard one blast from the *Pinthis'* whistle. The helmsman of the much larger *Fairfax* tried to turn his ship away as the engines were reversed. However, with her momentum still carrying her forward, the liner cut into the tanker 30 seconds later. Almost immediately, the *Pinthis* burst into flames. Blazing oil and gasoline flew into the air, raining flaming fuel down on both ships. The *Pinthis'* crew of 19 never had a chance—there were no survivors.

The *Fairfax's* captain tried to back his ship out of the burning tanker, but he could not until the *Pinthis* slowly pulled away as she sank. By this time, with the sky raining fire, the liner's forward decks were also in flames. Her captain quickly maneuvered his ship into the lee, preventing the roaring flames from spreading. Also, the crew, with help from U.S Navy seamen and Marines who were passengers, started to battle the blaze. A few passengers rushing onto the deck, however, perished in the flames. Others panicked and jumped over the side. Even some crew-members followed suit. Most were leaping to their deaths.

Although the *Pinthis* had sunk to the bottom, she was still a raging inferno, with oil and gasoline escaping her holds. The surface of the sea was covered with flames. Many fleeing the burning *Fairfax* died in these flames, others drowned because they had no life preservers to keep them afloat.

The fires aboard the liner were eventually extinguished by the combined efforts of crew and passengers, and she made it back to port under her own power.

The disaster, however, claimed the lives of 17 passengers and 11 of her crew. Combined with the 19 who perished aboard the *Pinthis*, a total of 47 drowned or were burned to death. Persons who experienced the inferno will never forget the experience, especially those who leaped into the flaming sea and survived. The tanker, lying in 100 feet of water, fed the flames for several days.

The *Pinthis* capsized as she sank and is keel up on a sand and gravel bottom. Her hull is almost intact except the bow is sheared off. Her engine, bolted to the hull and hanging upside down, broke loose after decades of extreme pressure on the engine mounts. The hull partly collapsed before the mounts separated, releasing the engine.

The tanker's screw was removed with explosives after World War II. The salvors thought that the screw was bronze, but it turned out to be steel. The explosion left a huge hole in the stern and since the wreck is upside down, a diver can penetrate where the shaft alley was and swim into the engine room. There are several other openings into the hull that allow easy penetration.

The superstructure collapsed as the *Pinthis* struck the bottom upside down. Its remains are scattered on the starboard side.

Visibility is usually good, sometimes exceeding 40 feet, and this wreck still yields many fine artifacts.

Brian Carter kneeling on the tanker's stern. Photo by the author.

The ship's steam whistle. Photo by Brian Skerry.

The finding and recovery of the *Pinthis'* steam whistle was a Carter family affair. Bill found it and Rusty (shown here) and Brian helped their father retrieve it. Photo by Brian Skerry.

The organ-pipe steam whistle required several months to clean and preserve but was in working order when the project was finished. The following summer the Carters used the whistle to celebrate the Fourth of July. Photo by Brian Skerry.

## 17. Lost in the "Portland Gale"—*Delaware*

| | |
|---|---|
| **Type of vessel** | : schooner barge |
| **Gross tons** | : 2,461 |
| **Length** | : 318.4 feet |
| **Beam** | : 35.6 feet |
| **Hull construction** | : iron |
| **Location** | : Collamore Ledge, Cohasset, MA |
| **Approximate depth of water:** | 30–65 feet |

On November 27, 1898, the convergence of two storm systems produced New England's most destructive blizzard. The terrifying seas and raging winds of nearly 100 knots claimed several ships. The side-paddle-wheeler *Portland* was one of those lost. There were no survivors. The only passenger list was on board. It went down with the ship, but it is estimated that 157 died. Because of the tragedy, the storm was named in memory of the steamer.

When the *Delaware* foundered during the "Portland Gale" she was an unglamorous schooner barge under tow by the tugboat *Mars*. However, her early career had been far more respectable. She was built at Renfrew, Scotland in 1873 and launched as the passenger steamer *Pembroke*. Later, she was sold to a Spanish company and was renamed *Murciano*.

After a long and successful career as a passenger steamer, the aging ship was bought by an American company, Bartlett & Sheppard of Philadelphia, that converted her into a schooner barge. Her remaining days

The *Delaware* foundered with the loss of her entire crew. Sketch by Paul C. Morris.

Brian Carter peers into the more intact bow section of the schooner barge. Steel plates have fallen off the wreck, exposing angle iron ribs. Photo by Brian Skerry.

were spent as the *Delaware*, being towed up and down the coast loaded with coal, a far cry from her role as a passenger steamer.

On November 27, 1898, the *Delaware* and another schooner barge, the *Daniel I. Tenny*, en route from Newport News, Virginia to Boston with cargos of coal, were being towed by the tugboat *Mars*. The three vessels were in Boston Bay when they encountered gale force winds and heavy seas. Captain Miles of the tugboat found it impossible to continue towing the two schooner barges and signaled them to anchor. They were between Minot's Light and the lightship, and he thought they could hold on. The wind was blowing over 75 knots and a tremendous sea was running. A huge wave broke over the tug, smashing the pilothouse, flooding the cabin and filling the lower part of the vessel. However, the *Mars* survived the storm but her tow did not. The *Delaware* grounded and broke up near Collamore Ledge, Cohasset, Massachusetts. The *Tenny* was also lost. There were no survivors from either vessel.

The *Delaware*'s remains were classified as a navigational hazard and they were eventually dynamited. Wreckage lies broken and scattered in 30 to 65 feet of water. The bow, however, is more intact. Visibility is usually poor, six to seven feet. On occasion, however, it may range from 20 to 30 feet.

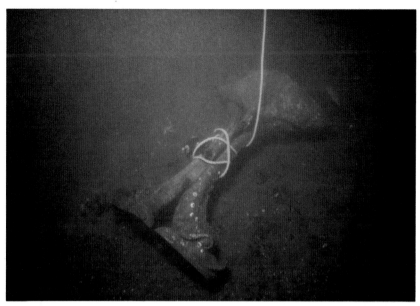

Brian Skerry found this compass binnacle on the *Delaware*. He attached the line and sent a marker to the surface before taking the photo.

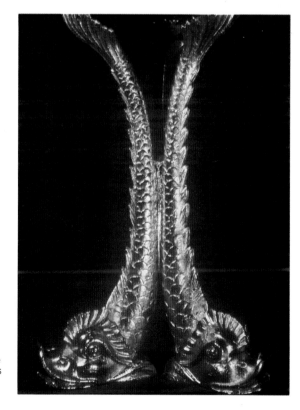

After cleaning and preservation, this beautiful artifact can be fully appreciated. The heads of the three brass dolphins functioned as a base, while their tails held the compass housing. Photo by Brian Skerry.

## 18. Run Down at Anchor—*Kiowa*

| | | |
|---|---|---|
| **Type of vessel** | : | freighter |
| **Gross tons** | : | 2,949 |
| **Length** | : | 291.2 feet |
| **Beam** | : | 43.1 feet |
| **Hull construction** | : | steel |
| **Location** | : | off Point Allerton, MA |
| **Lat. and long.** | : | 42–19.19 N, 70–51.52 W |
| **Approximate depth of water:** | | 45 feet |

The Clyde Line freighter had been in service only about nine months when she was lost in a collision just outside Boston Harbor. The steam-powered *Kiowa* had been built by Cramp & Sons at Philadelphia. She was a two-masted schooner-rigged steel vessel with three decks, considered one of the finest steam schooners on the East Coast.

The *Kiowa* was on her 13th voyage between Charleston, South Carolina and Boston with a cargo of 400,000 feet of hard pine, cotton, iron, wool, clay, and naval stores.

On the morning of December 26, 1903 she was approaching the entrance to Boston Harbor. The freighter had been fighting strong winds, heavy seas and blinding snow squalls all night. Under such conditions, her captain thought it unwise to try to enter the harbor, and gave orders to anchor. The *Kiowa* was off Point Allerton, one mile from the entrance to

The *Huron*, a sistership of the *Kiowa*. Photo courtesy of the Steamship Historical Society Collection, Univ. of Baltimore.

Boston Harbor. Because of the raging snowstorm, the heavy seas and the icy spray covering the vessel from stem to stern, most of the officers and crew who were not needed on deck were below. or under cover of some kind.

While the crew of the *Kiowa* was seeking shelter from the storm, the United Fruit Company's steel-hulled steamship *Admiral Dewey* was outbound from the harbor. She proceeded at slow speed, feeling her way with utmost caution. The passenger/freighter made her way out through the torturous narrows and by Boston Light without incident. It was close to noon, but visibility was very bad because of the wind-driven snow. However, the *Admiral Dewey*'s captain thought his ship was out of danger until, about a mile past the light, the *Kiowa* loomed up out of a snow squall, directly in his path.

The *Admiral Dewey* struck the anchored ship on her port side. She probably would have cut half-way through the *Kiowa*, but her steel bow struck the timber cargo, slowing the penetration. The stricken vessel, however, was doomed. Heeling under the blow and impetus of the *Admiral Dewey*, the *Kiowa* listed severely to starboard. Her frightened crew feared she would capsize and they would be trapped below. The grinding of steel plates, crunching of the lumber in the hold, and the pounding of waves on her partly submerged deck added to their fear. Surprisingly, no one on either vessel was injured.

As the *Admiral Dewey* backed away from her, the freighter righted, and her frightened crew rushed on deck. There was a gaping hole in the *Kiowa*'s side, through which water was pouring in great quantities. Her captain ordered water-tight bulkhead hatches to be closed and issued distress signals with the ship's whistle.

A tugboat, a quarter of a mile away, responded to the signals—but with caution. In the driving snow storm, her captain could not see the two freighters at first; before proceeding far, however, he sighted them. As the tug approached, the *Admiral Dewey* started off down the bay, apparently satisfied she was in no danger, and rescue was nearby for the crew of the sinking vessel. The *Admiral Dewey* had been built five years before in the same shipyard that had produced her victim.

The storm was at its height, complicating the rescue operation. The tug was brought in as close in the lee of the freighter as her captain dared in the terrific sea that was running. One by one, the crew of 31 was transferred, the officers being the last to abandon ship.

The *Kiowa* sank by her stern in 45 feet of water, leaving her smoke stack and masts above the surface. Two days after the disaster, the sails and rigging were removed, and a diver determined that damage to the hull was too severe to allow the ship to be raised.

Some of the freighter's wreckage came ashore at North Scituate beach. Most of it was of no value, but part of the *Kiowa*'s bridge reached shore and held the ship's compass. The sunken vessel, lying directly in the approaches to Boston Harbor, was a serious menace to navigation. She was blown apart by dynamite.

The wreckage, consisting primarily of steel ribs and plates, is flattened out on the bottom. However, in some areas it extends to ten feet above the bottom. The visibility is usually not very good, averaging only 15 feet, but the wreck is good for lobstering.

The Clyde Line freighter *Kiowa* after being run down by the *Dewey*. Photo courtesy of Richard M. Boonisar.

An elaborate brass
chandelier from the *Kiowa*,
recovered, preserved and
photographed by Bill Carter.

Brian Carter inspects a "come along" left attached to the wreck by other divers. Photo by
the author.

## 19. Zoo Wreck—*City of Salisbury*

| | | |
|---|---|---|
| **Type of vessel** | : | freighter |
| **Gross tons** | : | 5,924 |
| **Length** | : | 419 feet |
| **Beam** | : | 54 feet |
| **Hull construction** | : | steel |
| **Location** | : | Graves Ledge, NE of Graves Lighthouse |
| **Lat. and long.** | : | 42–22.26 N, 70–51.35 W |
| **Approximate depth of water:** | | 20–90 feet |

Bound from Calcutta, India to Boston, the British freighter *City of Salisbury* was within sight of Boston Harbor when she was engulfed by dense fog. The freighter struck an uncharted pinnacle of rock on Graves Ledge, just northeast of Graves Lighthouse, and drove hard aground on April 22, 1938. The pinnacle projects to within 22 feet of the surface at mean low water. Efforts to save her failed, but all 56 of her crew and most of her cargo survived.

Because of her exotic cargo, the freighter soon became known as the "Zoo Wreck." The cargo, assessed at one and one half million dollars, was worth almost three times the value of the steamer. In addition to rubber and bales of jute, large wicker containers held various species of birds, monkeys, pythons, deadly cobras, and other exotic animals. Some monkeys escaped during the disaster and scampered through the ship's rigging.

The *City of Salisbury* on Graves Ledge. Her back is broken and the bow is underwater. Note the excursion boat in the background. Photo courtesy of the Peabody Museum of Salem.

One large snake, badly decomposed, washed ashore and was mistaken for a sea serpent by the local population.

The *City of Salisbury*, built at Sunderland, England in 1924 for Ellerman Lines, Ltd., became a popular tourist attraction during the summer of 1938. Enterprising charter-boat captains out of Boston ran excursions to the "Zoo Wreck." However, that lasted only one summer. The constant action of passing swells tipping the ship back and forth like a pendulum, as well as the weight of the ship itself, broke the freighter in half, and she settled on both sides of the rocky ledge.

The pinnacle of rock is now known as "Salisbury Pinnacle." The wreck consists primarily of broken and scattered steel plates, with debris spread over the bottom at a depth of 20 to 90 feet. There are only a few pieces large enough to partly penetrate. Some cargo of jute remains. Thousands of pounds of brass have been recovered, but large valves and many other artifacts remain to be retrieved. Visibility is usually poor.

A large python, washed ashore on Race Point Beach. The large snake was badly decomposed and first thought to be a sea serpent. Photo courtesy of Brad Luther.

Wreckage is scattered over Graves Ledge; Bill Carter looks into one of the larger pieces. Photo by the author.

The cage from a moisture-proof lamp was recovered by Bill Carter. Photo by Paul Sherman.

## 20. Nearly Sheared in Half—*Romance*

| | | |
|---|---|---|
| **Type of vessel** | : | excursion steamer |
| **Gross tons** | : | 1,240 |
| **Length** | : | 245 feet |
| **Beam** | : | 38 feet |
| **Hull construction** | : | steel |
| **Location** | : | south of Nahant, MA |
| **Lat. and long.** | : | 42–23.43 N, 70–51.46 W |
| **Approximate depth of water:** | | 85 feet |

The old excursion steamer *Romance* had been on the Boston to Provincetown, Cape Cod run for only a year, but she already had a reputation for speed. The steamer's captain, Adelbert Wickens, had acquired one for recklessness.

The traveling public seems always to have been enamored of speed: in ships, in trains, in cars, in planes. The fascination of speed helped to develop rivalries between steamships.

The Boston to Provincetown excursion during summer weekends was a lucrative run, with the steamers competing for about 1,500 passengers. The *Romance*'s main rival was the *Steel Pier*. The passage across Massachusetts Bay often turned into a race between the two steamers. After

The excursion steamer *Romance*. Photo courtesy of The Peabody Museum of Salem.

one such competition, Captain Wickens of the *Romance* was called before the U.S. Bureau of Marine Inspection and Navigation, charged with "misbehavior, negligence, willful violation of the rules of the sea and endangering lives and property."

The steamer was built in 1898 at Wilmington, Delaware and christened the *Tennessee*. In 1935 the 37-year-old steamer was sold to the Bay State Steamship Company and began supplying passenger service between Boston and the Cape. Her new owners changed her name to *Romance*.

One year later, on September 9, 1936, the old excursion steamer was lost like many ships before her—in a dense fog. Because it was a weekday, only 208 passengers were on board for the one-day excursion to Cape Cod. The return trip was uneventful until the *Romance* reached Graves Lighthouse at the entrance to Boston Harbor, where she was engulfed by fog.

Captain Wickens knew the passenger liner *New York* was due to be coming out of Boston Harbor on her way to New York. Shortly before 7 p.m. he ordered the *Romance*'s speed reduced from 15 to 4 knots. The steamer's lookout was inexperienced and her wireless operator, who might have contacted the approaching passenger liner, had missed the boat that day.

Suddenly, the giant bow of the *New York* appeared out of the fog—less than 50 feet away, and approaching fast. She was on the *Romance*'s

The *New York*'s steel bow cuts into the *Romance*. The smaller excursion steamer would sink within 20 minutes of the collision. Sketch by Chris Hugo.

port side, and Captain Wickens ordered hard to starboard—a fatal mistake. When there is imminent danger of collision, two vessels should turn toward each other, decreasing the chance of a direct blow. Instead, Captain Wickens presented his vessel broadside to the other's bow. The Bureau of Marine Inspection would later suspend Wicken's license for six months for that action.

The *New York*'s steel bow nearly sheared the *Romance* in half. The liner's captain kept his vessel wedged into the *Romance*'s hull while his crew lowered rope ladders and cargo nets to the deck of the stricken ship. Although the *Romance*'s officers called for women and children first, most of the crew and orchestra clawed their way to safety before the passengers. However, all were rescued and, surprisingly, only 17 people were injured.

As the *Romance* sank in 85 feet of water, her wooden deck houses floated free. A couple of months later the old steamer, not worth salvaging, was blown apart with explosives to eliminate it as a threat to other ships.

The wreck is about 2½ miles southeast of East Point, Nahant, her bow is relatively intact, but the rest of the hull is broken up and scattered. Her massive boilers provide an impressive sight rising from the piles of debris.

The wreck is on a mud bottom and visibility is usually poor. The *Romance*, however, produces many artifacts.

Bill Carter recovered this gas lamp which had been converted to electricity.

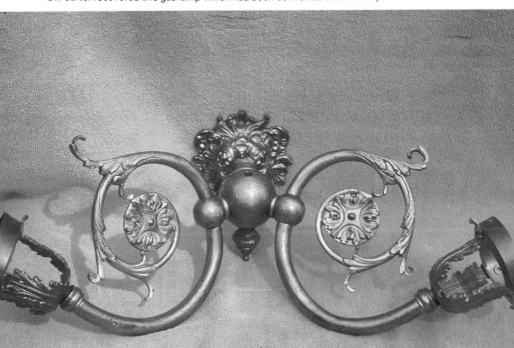

Steel wreckage covered
with sea anemones. Photo
by Bill Kurz.

## 21. Victim of Boo Hoo Ledge—*Albert Gallatin*

| | | |
|---|---|---|
| **Type of vessel** | : | revenue cutter |
| **Gross tons** | : | 250 |
| **Length** | : | 142 feet |
| **Beam** | : | 23 feet |
| **Hull construction** | : | iron |
| **Location** | : | Boo Hoo Ledge, Manchester, MA |
| **Approximate depth of water:** | | 15–50 feet |

During a violent gale the revenue cutter *Albert Gallatin* proved that a rocky ledge off Manchester, Massachusetts was appropriately named Boo Hoo Ledge.

The first Congress of the United States, in desperate need of operating funds for the fledgling republic, established a protective tariff. To enforce it, the Revenue Cutter Service was created under Alexander Hamilton in 1790. Officers were given military rank, and during the War of 1812 and the Civil War, cutters operated with the Navy. In 1837 Congress directed the Revenue Cutter Service to make "seasonal cruises along the coast for the relief of distressed mariners."

By Act of Congress on January 30, 1915, the Revenue Cutter Service and the Life-Saving Service became known as the Coast Guard Service, later the U.S. Coast Guard.

The revenue cutter *Albert Gallatin*. Photo courtesy of The Peabody Museum of Salem.

The *Albert Gallatin* was built during 1870 and 1871 at Buffalo, New York. The revenue cutter proved unsatisfactory during her trials, and alterations had to be made by the builder. She was finally accepted into service in October of 1874 and ordered to Boston. She continued on the Boston station as a revenue cutter, cruising the Massachusetts and New Hampshire coasts for almost 20 years. The only interruption occurred in 1887, when the two-masted steamer was ordered to New York for several months to receive a new boiler.

The *Gallatin* carried two brass cannons and some small arms. She was square-rigged for the summer and schooner-rigged for winter. Her complement was seven officers and 30 seamen. In November-December 1891, the cutter underwent a $10,000 overhaul.

On the morning of January 7, 1892, the *Gallatin* left Portsmouth, New Hampshire for Provincetown, Massachusetts. The east-south east wind was blowing fresh, and rising. Within three hours the winds had reached gale force and were accompanied by a blinding snow storm. The cutter's captain decided to run for Gloucester Harbor under reduced steam.

When land was sighted the cutter's pilot thought it was Kettle Island. He headed the *Gallatin* to what he thought was Eastern Point, for protection from the mounting seas. Within minutes the cutter struck Boo Hoo Ledge and water rushed into the ship.

The captain ordered "abandon ship," with seas breaking over his vessel and water pouring into the hull. While the first lifeboat was being lowered, the *Gallatin* lurched to port, tearing off the main top mast and smoke stack. The ship's carpenter was struck in the head by the falling stack and was instantly killed. His body fell overboard and was lost.

The lifeboats were launched with great difficulty because of the raging sea. They reached Singing Beach at Manchester, Massachusetts. Three boats, however, were destroyed by heavy rollers while landing, but no lives werre lost.

The crew lost all their clothing, money and jewelry, except what they wore. The loss of all their possessions left many destitute. After investigation of the sinking though they were not found to be at fault, the men were discharged from the service. A Board of Inquiry found the disaster was the result of an "Error in the Judgement of C.O."

Two months after the sinking, the Collector of Customs at Boston transferred the *Gallatin*'s title to three Boston men who intended to salvage the vessel. The cutter had been valued at $50,000 prior to her sinking; the winning bid for her remains was $679.

Today, the hull lies broken and scattered among huge rocks in from 15 to 50 feet of water. The rocks are surprisingly free from kelp. Many sea urchins are in the area and their spines can easily penetrate wet suits and gloves. Visibility is usually good, 25 to 30 feet.

Wreckage is scattered over the rock ledge, in crevices and gulleys. Photo by Paul Sherman.

On the left is a well-worn deck light from the *Gallatin*; a reproduction is on the right. Deck lights were set flush into the deck with the prism pointing into the cabin below so sunlight would be dispersed through the prism. The artifact was recovered by Bill Carter and photographed by Paul Sherman.

This brass letter from the revenue cutter's hull was retrieved by Bill Carter. Photo by Dave Clancy.

Artifacts recovered from the *Gallatin* and photographed by Bill Carter.

## 22. Last Ship-of-the-Line—USS *New Hampshire*

| | | |
|---|---|---|
| **Type of vessel** | : | warship |
| **Gross tons** | : | 2,633 |
| **Length** | : | 203.8 feet |
| **Beam** | : | 51.4 feet |
| **Hull construction** | : | wood |
| **Location** | : | Graves Island, Manchester, MA |
| **Approximate depth of water** | : | 10–40 feet |

The last surviving American ship-of-the-line was lost to the sea in July 1922. Congress had authorized her construction 106 years before.

On April 29, 1816 Congress authorized the construction of nine ships-of-the-line, each with no fewer than 74 guns. Funding of one million dollars a year for the next eight years was specified to assure that they would be built. Construction of the new warships was in government yards rather than in private shipyards because of the uncertainty of the eight-year funding.

Predictably, the economy dictated the completion schedules of the new ships. The powerful 74's would be held in readiness for launching only

Although her hull was pierced for 102 guns, the *New Hampshire* carried far fewer. Photo courtesy of The Peabody Museum of Salem.

as needed for national interests. For example, the *Alabama* was almost completed by 1825, but she remained on the stocks at the Portsmouth (N.H.) Navy Yard for an additional 39 years. She was under construction for 45 years—longer than the careers of many ships.

It took the Civil War to bring her into service. The warship was renamed the *New Hampshire*, which was considered more appropriate for service against the Confederacy. She was launched April 23, 1864 and commissioned the following month. Although her hull was pierced for 102 guns the *New Hampshire*'s original armament was four 100-pounder Parrott rifled and six 9-inch Dahlgren smooth-bore guns. She sailed to Port Royal, South Carolina to relieve her sister ship the *Vermont*, and served as a supply and hospital ship for the remainder of the war.

Beginning June 8, 1866 she served as a receiving ship at Norfolk, Virginia for ten years. On May 10, 1876 she returned to Port Royal, still a receiving ship. In 1881 she sailed to Norfolk for more of the same duty until ordered to Newport, Rhode Island, where the *New Hampshire* became the flagship of the newly formed Apprentice Training Squadron.

In 1893 the old ship-of-the-line was loaned to the New York State Naval Militia for use as a training ship and armory. Nearly a thousand officers and men who trained aboard her served in the Spanish-American War.

On November 30, 1904 the *New Hampshire* was renamed the *Granite State* to make her name available for a steam-powered, steel-hulled battleship.

Aboard the *New Hampshire* off Charleston, S.C. during the Civil War, a "powder monkey" stands beside a 100-pdr Parrott rifled gun. Photo courtesy of the Library of Congress.

For many years following the Civil War, the warship was used as a receiving ship. Photo courtesy of the National Archives.

In 1913 her career almost ended with a fire that spread rapidly through the forecastle and superstructure. Almost certain destruction was averted by timely flooding of the ship's magazines. Some of the crew were treated for smoke inhalation, but there were no serious injuries.

The old ship continued service as a training ship, stationed on the Hudson River, until another fire struck on May 23, 1921. This time the vessel did not fare as well as eight years earlier. A large pool of fuel oil had collected on the surface from a leaking six-inch Standard Oil pipeline under the river. At 3 p.m. three sailors in a Captain's gig came through the oil slick, approaching the pier to which the *Granite State* was moored. The gig's motor back-fired several times, shooting sparks and flame from the exhaust, igniting the fuel oil.

The sailors escaped, but not the old warship or the three-story naval office and storehouse on the Ninety-sixth Street pier. President Harding had landed at the pier that morning, but he was not near at the time and his yacht *Mayflower* was safely at anchor several hundred yards offshore.

Fire stations ashore could not be used to save the ship because of low water pressure. Firemen and two fire-boats were assisted by the ship's crew and those from other naval vessels in a valiant but unrewarding effort to save the ship. Only her mooring chains kept her from capsizing as she listed sharply to port and settled into the muddy river bottom, a smoldering hulk. The damage was estimated at $250,000, but there was never a thought of repair—her original cost was $304,533.85.

The Mulholland Machinery Corporation of New York bought the remains for $5,000 at auction in August 1921. After the sale, a brief military

ARMORY OF NAVAL MILITIA. U.S.S NEW HAMPSHIRE.

The old ship-of-the-line was converted into an armory for the naval militia. Photo courtesy of the Naval Historical Center.

ceremony ended with a bugler sounding taps to signal the end of the career for the U.S. Navy's last ship-of-the-line.

The new owners calculated that the hull contained $70,000 in salvageable materials. She was copper-fastened, and her hull of valuable hardwood was covered with 100 tons of copper sheathing. Rumor had it that somewhere in her keel she had three gold spikes. Her two anchors weighed five tons each, and she carried 100 tons of chain. There were even twelve pianos below deck, but they no longer were of value, even with the hull refloated.

Divers sealed the gun ports and patched holes in the hull with three layers of canvas before the ship was raised with pontoons. After five months to complete the operation, the *Granite State* was taken in tow in July 1922, bound for Eastport, Maine for removal of her copper fastenings.

Five days later, while under tow, the captain of the tug saw smoke rising from the bow of the hulk and supposed the men on board were cooking, but it was not cooking that raised the smoke. The old ship was fighting her third battle with fire. Flames spread rapidly, and the tug dropped back to take aboard the two-man crew, who had escaped the burning vessel in a rowboat. The original tow line tore loose from the flaming bow.

The tug stood by helplessly watching the burning ship drift until she stranded on the granite shore, off the southwest corner of Graves Island in Massachusetts Bay. The next morning local residents descended on the fire-ravaged hulk and appropriated huge quantities of her valuable metals. The wreck rested, abandoned and almost forgotten, while over the years storms battered the hull against the rocks until broken ribs and timbers were slowly covered with sand.

Thirty years passed before divers rediscovered the wreck. Since then salvagers have ravaged it three times. On each occasion they retrieved huge oak timbers with copper spikes and drift pins still attached. Those fastenings, an anchor, and many cannon balls that had been carried as ballast were sold for their metal content. What a pity it was to lose those historical artifacts.

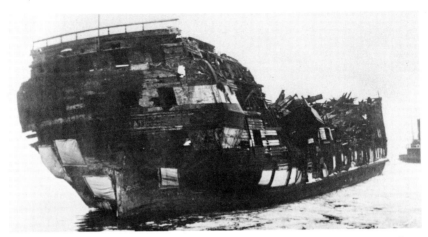

After burning and sinking in New York Harbor, the hulk was raised and was under tow when she sank in Massachusetts Bay. Photo courtesy of the Naval Historical Center.

The fastenings are believed to have been forged at the Paul Revere Foundry. Revere received a contract for a large quantity of copper spikes, drift pins, sheathing, and sheathing nails from the navy in 1816. The fittings are identical to those on the smaller *Constitution*, whose fittings were made by Revere.

Spikes used to hold planks in place measured six to twelve inches in length. Drift pins were longer and used as rods to reinforce the ship's structural members. The term "drift pin" comes from beating them into pre-drilled holes, called drifting.

Every dive on the *Granite State* becomes a new experience. She can be best described as "wreckage," rather than a wreck. Her remains are scattered about the bottom in 10 to 40 feet of water, with her giant curved ribs rising out of the sand. Storms continue to cover and uncover those ribs and other pieces to provide an ever-changing underwater panorama.

Accessibility is one of the truly attractive aspects of diving this wreck. The location, Graves Island, is just off shore from Graves Beach, Manchester, Massachusetts. One could walk from the beach to the island at low tide, but the shore next to the island is privately owned and access to the wreck must be made by boat. That poses no problem, particularly when seas are calm; the location is only three and one half miles down the coast from the entrance to Gloucester Harbor.

Although visibility varies, it is usually good. The shallow depth makes the wreck site suitable, even for the novice driver. But, in rough seas, the turbulence can create treacherous conditions, since the wreckage is so near the island's rocky shore.

This shipwreck, known by many as New England's most famous, received in the year of this country's bicentennial what was probably the USS *New Hampshire*'s greatest distinction: its acceptance into the National Register of Historic Places.

A diver swims to the wreck site off Graves Island. Photo by the author.

A drift pin sticks out of a ship's timber. Photo by Paul Sherman.

The *New Hampshire*'s
copper fastenings are often
encrusted onto the rocks.
Bill Carter is using a hammer
and chisel to dig out a spike.
Photo by Paul Sherman.

An assortment of copper fastenings recovered from the *New Hamsphire* by Bill Carter. The spike in the center is stamped with "U.S." Photo by Dave Clancy.

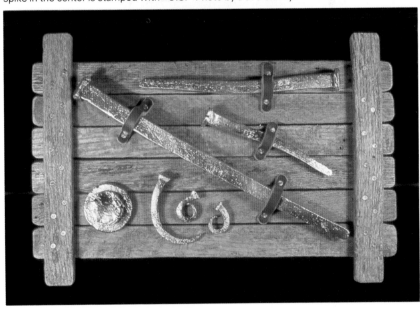

A scabbard buckle and two other artifacts recovered and photographed by Bill Carter.

An elaborate pressure reducing valve off the wreck. It was found in this quartered condition by Bill Carter. Obviously, the valve was used for demonstration purposes as a teaching aid. Photo by Paul Sherman.

## 23. Thirty-Foot Seas Split Tanker in Half—*Chester A. Poling*

| | | |
|---|---|---|
| **Type of vessel** | : | coastal tanker |
| **Length** | : | 281.4 feet |
| **Beam** | : | 40 feet |
| **Hull construction** | : | steel |
| **Location** | : | 1500 yards off Glouscester breakwater |
| **Lat. and long.** | : | 42–34.7 N, 70–40.3 W |
| **Approximate depth of water:** | | 95 feet |

The aging coastal tanker *Chester A. Poling* had unloaded her cargo of heating oil at the Exxon terminal in Everett, Massachusetts and was to return to Newington, New Hampshire. The tanker's captain, Charles H. Burgess, had received a weather forecast calling for winds increasing from 35 to 45 knots and seas building to 6 to 10 feet. What the *Poling* actually encountered on the morning of January 10, 1977 was 65-knot winds and 30-foot seas.

The tanker had been built at Staten Island, New York in 1934 and christened *Plattsburg Scocony*. Later she was sold and her name was changed to *Mobil Albany*. In 1956 the tanker was sold to Poling Transportation Corporation and renamed *Chester A. Poling*.

The old tanker, in ballast, was taking a terrific pounding from mountainous seas as she headed for New Hampshire. Six miles off Cape Ann,

In 1956, the *Mobil Albany* was sold to the Poling Transportation Corporation and renamed the *Chester A. Poling*. Photo courtesy of Bill Carter.

Seaman Harry Selleck heard an unfamiliar sound. He later stated, "I heard a large bang like a piece of steel hitting the deck." Captain Burgess slowed the *Poling*'s speed and Selleck went on deck to investigate but did not see anything out of the ordinary. Burgess then increased speed and a second loud noise followed. The tanker started to "seasaw" according to Selleck and he watched with horror as the starboard side of the bow bent back to the starboard side of the stern, banged together a couple of times, then parted.

The gale-force winds and 30-foot seas had split the *Poling* in half. Burgess and Selleck were on the bow and the other five crew members were on the stern.

While the wind and sea pushed the two halves toward shore, Captain Burgess sent out a "Mayday." The distress call was quickly picked up by a Coast Guard cutter and relayed to the Gloucester Coast Guard station.

Slashing, intermittent rain and snow had reduced visibility to about 100 yards. The Coast Guard, however, sent a helicopter to search for the *Poling*—it was a life or death situation. Also, two small boats were sent out, a 41-footer and a 44-footer, each with four-man crews. Once they were clear of the Gloucester breakwater the small boats were "thrown around like toys." Almost overmatched by the stormy seas, the boats plowed toward the broken and sinking tanker.

An 18-year-old seaman, in the 41-footer, was knocked down by a large wave, injuring his back. In the other boat a 21-year-old seaman was thrown against a bulkhead, knocking him unconscious and injuring his arm. Both boats continued their rescue operation and reached the *Poling*. By the time they arrived, the helicopter and the 95-foot Coast Guard cutter *Cape Cross* had managed to save all except one of the tanker's crew.

Captain Burgess and Selleck, on the bow section, were rescued by the cutter after leaping into the water. A helicopter crewman lowered a rescue basket, from a height of only 20 feet, to the five men on the stern. One of the men was safely hoisted up but the next man, the ship's cook, was lost. As the basket was being lowered for him the cook made a desperate leap, but missed and plunged into the 30-degree water. He did not have a life jacket or survival suit on. A Coast Guard helicopter crewman later reported, "He seemed okay when he first came up (from underwater). We dropped the basket into the water as close to him as we could." The wind or sea, however, pulled the basket away from the swimming cook, who then managed to get within an arm's reach of his shipmates on the tanker's stern. The helicopter crewman later stated, "A wave broke over the man. I don't know whether he swallowed water or what, but when he came up he was face down in the water spreadeagled." The body disappeared.

Before the rescue basket could be lowered again, a large wave struck the stern, throwing the remaining three men into the water. Two were picked up by the Coast Guard cutter and the other by the helicopter.

The *Poling*'s bow section sank about four miles off Eastern Point in approximately 190 feet of water. The stern section remained afloat and drifted to a point 800 yards from the breakwater at Gloucester where it sank in about 75 feet of water.

The National Transportation Board reported, almost two years later, that the sinking of the *Poling* was the result of six contributing factors:

— Structural failure
— The effects of the high seas on the ship
— Improper ballasting of the empty tanker
— Excessive speed
— The lack of a loading manual
— Inaccurate National Weather Service storm forecast

A cargo hold amidship had been left without ballest and in the heavy seas a structural defect in the tanker's hull caused a buckling of the bottom plates.

Huges seas produced by the 'Blizzard of 1978' moved the stern section several hundred yards into deeper water. The intact stern is sitting upright on a sand and gravel bottom in about 95 feet of water.

Sport divers as well as commercial salvors have stripped the *Poling* and few artifacts can still be found. Most of the hatches are open and allow penetration for the experienced diver, using proper safety precautions.

Usually visibility is very good (20 to 50 feet) and there is little current to contend with. On a day with poor visibility, however, it is possible to swim, without realizing it, inside the cavernous cargo hold where the tanker split.

The *Poling*'s stern is Cape Ann's most popular wreck and is an impressive dive. Not often does a diver see an almost intact wreck sitting upright on the bottom.

Side scan sonar printout of the *Poling*'s aft section. Courtesy of EG & G.

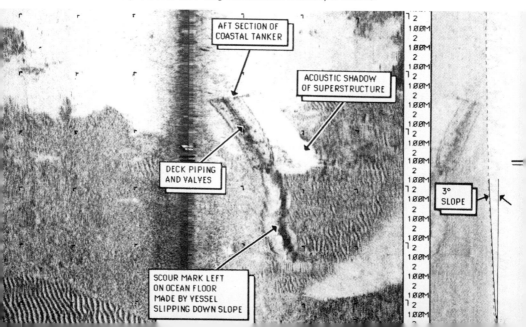

When divers first visited the wreck there was no doubt regarding the ship's name. Photo by Paul Sherman.

Rusty Carter removing a sign from a piece of deck machinery. Photo by Paul Sherman.

Inside the *Poling*'s galley. In the photo below, a pot still sits on the stove and a box of tea can be seen behind it. Photos by Paul Sherman.

Several years later marine organisms have taken up residence on the wreck. Photos by Chip Cooper.

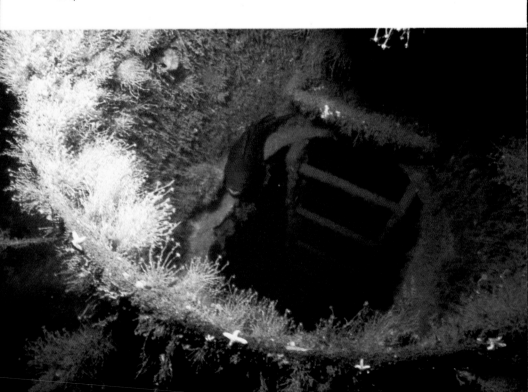

# 24. Hollywood Wreck—*Chelsea*

| | | |
|---|---|---|
| **Type of vessel** | : | coastal tanker |
| **Gross tons** | : | 556 |
| **Length** | : | 169.7 feet |
| **Beam** | : | 30.1 feet |
| **Hull construction** | : | steel |
| **Location** | : | 1,400 yards northeast of Thatchers Island |
| **Lat. and long.** | : | 42–38.52 N, 70–34.11 W |
| **Approximate depth of water:** | | 45–60 feet |

The small coastal oil tanker was not very pretty before she sank, but she has since become a beautiful shipwreck. The tanker struck a submerged section of the Sandy Bay Breakwater, off Rockport, Massachusetts, Sunday afternoon, February 10, 1957. The tanker had been built in 1919 at Bath, Maine for Texaco and christened *Texaco 145*, but was later sold to Peerless Number One Corporation, which renamed her *Chelsea*. The old tanker was traveling from her homeport of Boston to Newington, New Hampshire with 6,500 barrels of fuel oil. The same day the *Chelsea* went aground, she was pulled off by the U.S. Coast Guard cutter *Evergreen* and set adrift. While the tanker drifted, the Coast Guard managed to get two tow lines to her. However, while under tow, 1,400 yards 20 degrees true from Thatchers Island Light, the *Chelsea* capsized and sank rapidly. Only

She was not exceptionally pretty before her sinking, but the *Chelsea* has become a beautiful shipwreck. Photo courtesy of The Peabody Museum of Salem.

quick action by the Coast Guard saved the *Evergreen*: the tow lines were severed with an axe. The cutter escaped being dragged down with the tanker, and the *Chelsea*'s crew of six were plucked from the sea.

The tanker struck a rock ledge and righted herself as she settled in 45 to 60 feet of water with her forward section resting on a smaller rock ledge and her aft section in the sand. Plans to salvage the *Chelsea* were abandoned when her mid-section, which was not supported, split in two, releasing her cargo of fuel oil. Rockport's shoreline was saved from pollution by the prevailing offshore winds that carried the escaping oil out to sea.

Many divers refer to the *Chelsea* as the "Hollywood Wreck" because the forward section is intact and in an upright position. Many shipwrecks have been blown apart with explosives because they were navigational hazards, or they have been beaten down by the sea. Such wrecks resemble a junkyard rather than a ship. The *Chelsea*'s stern is broken up and scattered over the bottom. The bow section, however, is a beautiful sight lying beside a large kelp-covered rock ledge. The ledge has protected that part of the wreck from the destructive force of severe storms.

Several places in the intact forward section, including a companionway hatch, allow easy penetration. The *Chelsea*'s interior is open, with only a few steel beams to swim around. Sunlight filters down through the deck to provide a beautiful sight that is at the same time eerie. It is strange to experience the blending of sky and undersea life. Visibility is usually good and the *Chelsea* is ideal for photography.

Rusty Carter on the cutting edge of the *Chelsea*'s bow. Photo by Brian Skerry.

After removing some marine growth on the bow, divers exposed raised, white painted letters identifying the tanker. The letters, cast in iron and not brass, were left on the wreck. Photos by Brian Skerry.

Rusty Carter swims through the tanker's intact bow. Photo by Brian Skerry.

Several openings in the intact bow allow easy penetration. Tom Molloy poses in the kelp-surrounded companionway that leads below. Photo by the author.

# 25. Liberty Ship—*Charles S. Haight*

| | | |
|---|---|---|
| **Type of vessel** | : | freighter |
| **Gross tons** | : | 7,198 |
| **Length** | : | 422.8 feet |
| **Beam** | : | 57 feet |
| **Hull construction** | : | steel |
| **Location** | : | off the Sandy Bay Breakwater, Rockport, MA |
| **Approximate depth of water:** | | 15–45 feet |

The *Charles S. Haight* is one of the largest group of ships ever to be constructed from a single design—the Liberty ship.

At the beginning of World War II, Britain was inclined to make light of the U-boat threat. Relatively low shipping losses ealry in the war contributed to that complacency.

With the fall of France on June 22, 1940, the entire strategic balance changed. Germany had gained ports to base her U-boats along occupied France's 2,500 mile ocean front. U-boats no longer had the long voyage north around the British Isles to reach the shipping lanes without encountering minefields. Allied shipping losses increased rapidly.

In September 1940, a British delegation contracted with Henry J. Kaiser to build 60 badly needed freighters. United States shipyards were swamped with work, so they had to turn to a man who had built dams and bridges—but not ships. Kaiser said he could do it and he did. He turned the mudflats of Richmond, California into a shipyard which built 30 of the freighters. The remainder were built at Portland, Maine.

The *Charles S. Haight* aground and broken in half off Rockport's breakwater. Photo courtesy of Bill Carter.

Even though the United States was still a neutral in early 1941, President Franklin Roosevelt became alarmed over shipping losses in the "Battle of the Atlantic." He directed the Maritime Commission to mass produce freighters. The Commission picked the British design, but chose oil as a fuel instead of coal; where the British split the deckhouse, it was left intact.

As the war progressed and the United States was drawn into the conflict, prefabrication and assembly went on around the clock. Production time was shortened from about seven months per ship to about one month, often to only weeks.

More than 2,700 of these freighters were built at shipyards all along the U.S. coast. They were called Liberty ships because they ferried supplies in support of the "fight for liberty."

The Liberty ships were slow (11 knots), easy prey for U-boats, and expendable, since they were being produced in such quantity. On D-day, several were scuttled to form a breakwater to protect landing sites.

President Roosevelt, seeing the design for the first time, dubbed the ship the "ugly duckling." Although they were slow and not very pretty to some, they were rugged and dependable.

By April 1946 the war had been won, but our former Allies in Europe still needed food and other supplies. The *Charles S. Haight*, which had been built at Brunswick, Georgia in 1944, was in ballast, bound for Boston from Newport, England.

On April 2, the freighter was driven wide from her course by a blinding southeast snow storm. She went ashore off Rockport, Massachusetts. Her stern was fast on a rocky ledge, known as Flat Ground, 500 yards northeast of the northern tip of the Sandy Bay Breakwater. Several U.S. Navy and Coast Guard vessels and a commercial salvage tug were dispatched to lend assistance in pulling the *Haight* off the rocks.

The freighter's captain and crew of 49 men remained on board as the ship appeared to be in no danger and the storm was abating. Her pumps were handling the incoming water from a leak in the stern. However, the following day the crew was removed. Then on April 4, salvage vessels tried to float the *Haight* and found her hull badly cracked. Two days later she broke in half.

Although the freighter was extensively salvaged, then dynamited, there is much wreckage scattered over the rocky bottom. Most is covered with kelp in about 15 feet of water. Sections of the bow are intact in 40–45 feet of water. With the engine awash at low tide, the wreck is easily located. It is indicated on local charts with a wreck symbol. The bow section is about one-half the distance between the breakwater and the engine. Visibility averages 20 feet, but during certain tides a strong current flows over the wreck.

The freighter was extensively salvaged, then dynamited, but the engine is awash at low tide. Photo by the author.

Inside the massive triple expansion engine. Photo by the author.

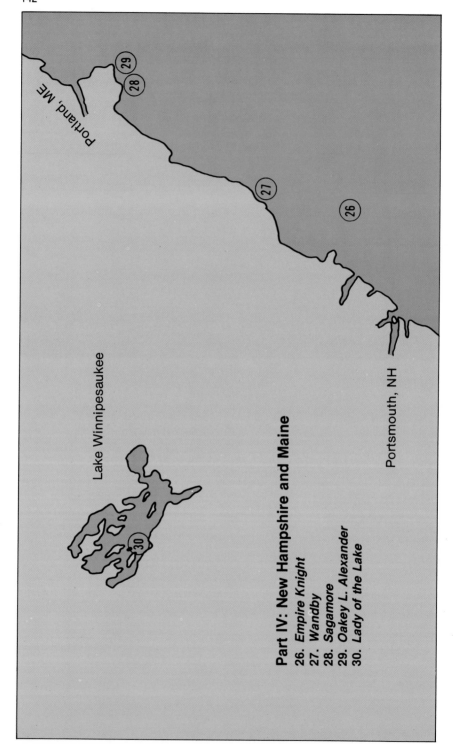

Portland, ME

Lake Winnipesaukee

Part IV: New Hampshire and Maine

26. *Empire Knight*
27. *Wandby*
28. *Sagamore*
29. *Oakey L. Alexander*
30. *Lady of the Lake*

Portsmouth, NH

# 26. Valuable Cargo—*Empire Knight*

| | | |
|---|---|---|
| **Type of vessel** | : | freighter |
| **Gross tons** | : | 7,244 |
| **Length** | : | 428.3 feet |
| **Beam** | : | 56.5 feet |
| **Hull construction** | : | steel |
| **Location** | : | Boon Island Ledge, off York, ME |
| **Lat. and long.** | : | 43–07.64 N, 70–24.90 W |
| **Approximate depth of water:** | | 20–120 feet |

The Second World War had raged for more than four years when the two-year-old British freighter *Empire Knight* picked up her cargo at St. John, New Brunswick en route to India via New York. Although the freighter was armed and boasted Royal Navy gunners, her crew still felt their greatest threat was German U-boats. However, on the afternoon of February 11, 1944, a northeaster proved to be their undoing.

In a blinding snowstorm and gale force winds of over 40 knots with gusts to 60 knots, a light was sighted a half-mile to a mile off the port beam. The *Empire Knight*'s captain recognized it to be the lighted whistle buoy marking Boon Island Ledge off York, Maine. The rocky ledge comes to within 10 feet of the surface. He knew the light should have been to starboard and his ship was in shoal water and in danger. He quickly reduced speed and headed the freighter northward, hoping to regain open water. It was too late, however, and the *Empire Knight* struck the ledge.

Distress signals attracted several rescue vessels, but with heavy seas crashing over the freighter's deck there was nothing they could do. The ship was continuously battered by waves. All except one liferaft was torn loose and two of the three lifeboats were smashed. At midnight the temperature was three degrees above zero, and winds were a steady 55 to 60 knots. The wind-driven spray and intense cold was encasing the ship in ice.

The following morning the signal was given to abandon ship. When the one remaining lifeboat was lowered with three men, it immediately capsized in the rough seas. The captain of the U.S. Navy minesweeper *Firm*, which had been standing by during the night with several other Navy and Coast Guard vessels, sent three rubber-suited divers after the helpless seamen. Without survival suits, life expectancy in those deathly cold conditions was short.

The pounding and lashing seas broke off the *Empire Knight*'s after two-thirds. Only the freighter's bow section was fast on the ledge. Her midships and stern were in open water. The heavy seas had weakened the ship's hull, and she buckled and broke about 115 feet from the bow, throwing cargo and crew into the sea. The after section drifted off and was quickly obscured in a snow squall.

When the *Empire Knight* broke in half, much of her cargo fell into the sea. The freighter's bow is shown here grounded on Boon Island Ledge. Photo courtesy of the National Archives.

The rescue vessels immediately went into action to pick up survivors. Twenty of the *Empire Knight*'s crew were saved, but 24, including the captain, lost their lives in the disaster.

Thirteen bodies were recovered, and the rescue vessels searched in vain for the after section in hope that it had remained afloat with survivors still on board. It was finally concluded that the stern must have sunk shortly after floating away. The recovered bodies were buried with full military honors at the Portsmouth Navy Yard cemetery.

The search for the stern continues today because of the value of her cargo. The *Empire Knight* was carrying military supplies for the war effort. The Ministry of Transport lists the main items of cargo as:

Military 2,400 tons
Ammunition 88 tons
Copper ingots 350 tons
Whiskey 5 tons
Commercial priority 1,300 tons

Military vechicles 2,300 tons
Government cargo 3,300 tons
Locomotives 400 tons
Ammonium Sulphate 2,000 tons

No additional information was given regarding the cargo classified as military, ammunition, government and non-government. Some of the unspecified cargo is thought to be industrial diamonds and Canadian currency. The diamonds, currency, and copper ingots would make this a valuable cargo to salvage.

When the *Empire Knight* broke in two, cargo fell out and scattered over the bottom. Piles of it are still present, but no one has found copper ingots or other valuable materials. They are probably still in the yet-to-be-discovered two-thirds of the freighter. The bow section remained on the ledge for several years until a severe stormed washed her off and under.

Boon Island Ledge is about 13 miles from the mainland and three miles off Boon Island, a desolate island containing only a lighthouse. This area is the scene of 35 documented shipwrecks. Large granite blocks from a schooner that sank 50 years before the freighter are scattered among the remains and cargo of the *Empire Knight*.

Pieces of wreckage and cargo are strewn over an area of about three acres, where water depth ranges from about 20 feet to approximately 120 feet. Most of the wreckage and cargo is in protected waters on the mainland side of the ledge. The anchor, in about 55 feet of water, is still fastened to a steel plate. Visibility is usually good, but occasionally there are strong currents and a surge. The wreck site is beautiful, with large specimens of kelp and other marine organisms growing on and around the wreckage.

Jon Bartley inspects a large shell casing. Photo by Gary Carbonneau.

Ordnance, part of the cargo, is scattered among the remains of the freighter. Jon Bartley finds a projectile and holds it for Gary Carbonneau to photograph. The stipes of Kelp are as large as steel cables.

Jon Bartley inside the cabin of a locomotive, part of the cargo. Photo by Gary Carbonneau.

Steve Bielenda holds a grinding stone Jim Dolph recovered from the *Empire Knight*. There are many of these grinding stones on the wreck, but because of possible hairline fractures, it would be unwise to try to use them. Photo by the author.

## 27. Full Speed Ahead—*Wandby*

| | | |
|---|---|---|
| **Type of vessel** | : | freighter |
| **Gross tons** | : | 3,980 |
| **Length** | : | 336.5 feet |
| **Beam** | : | 46.5 feet |
| **Hull construction** | : | steel |
| **Lat. and long.** | : | 43–20.11 N, 70–30.42 W |
| **Location** | : | Walker's Point, Keenebunkport, ME |
| **Approximate depth of water:** | | 5–35 feet |

For three days a dense fog had impeded New England shipping. The masters of most ships were slowly feeling their way around the treacherous rocky coast of Maine. The captain of the British freighter *Wandby*, however, was steaming full speed ahead when his ship ran aground off Walker's Point, near the little fishing village and summer resort of Kennebunkport, Maine.

Captain David Simpson was reduced to first mate following the disaster. He worked his way back to captain and during World War II was lost when his ship was sunk by a German U-boat.

The aging *Wandby*, built in 1899 in England for Ropner Shipping Company, had an interesting career, steaming to the far corners of the world. During World War I the *Wandby* rammed and sank a U-boat.

On one occasion, the freighter was long overdue and presumed lost. Her owners collected insurance on the ship and memorial services were held for the crew. However, the *Wandby*, which had been delayed by drifting ice floes in the White Sea, finally made her way above the Arctic Circle, around hazardous North Cape, and eventually to port.

On March 9, 1921 the freighter was bound for Portland, Maine from Algiers, North Africa. She was in ballast and was to take on a cargo of grain. Just before 10 a.m., Captain Simpson stopped his ship by a buoy and tried to decipher its markings in the enshrouding fog. Finally, he pronounced that they were on course, only 40 miles due east of their destination, Portland. He then ordered 'full ahead.' Actually, the freighter was about 20 miles south of Portland, steaming at top speed directly toward the rocky coast only about a mile away. The *Wandby* struck rocks with such a resounding crash that the sound was heard at Cape Porpoise, nearly two miles away. The local residents first thought it was thunder, but distress signals from the freighter quickly corrected that impression.

The freighter's frightened crew of 29 had no idea where they had grounded. They could hear booming breakers, but the ship could have struck an exposed rock ledge several miles offshore. If that were the case, the *Wandby* could break in two and carry them under with her. Later, the men could hear muffled voices and, when the fog lifted around 3 p.m., they found to their surprise that the *Wandby*'s bow was high and dry on the beach.

The *Wandby* hard aground off Walker's Point. Photo courtesy of Jim Dolph.

Fascinated spectators strolled the beach waiting for developments. The local fishermen were astounded that the freighter's officers had not seen the Boon Island Light to the south, even in the peasoup fog, or heard the fog horn and bell buoy off Cape Porpoise, just to the north.

The freighter was heavily salvaged. Photo from the collection of The Brick Store Museum.

Most shipwrecks generated much excitement for the local population, but the stranded *Wandby* was a larger attraction than usual. The trolley line was only two miles distant, providing easy access. Many people from Portland to Portsmouth visited and photographed the old freighter in her humiliating predicament. Special trolley cars were run from Seaford and Biddeford the weekend after the *Wandby* stranded. Between 4,000 and 5,000 people visited Kennebunkport and the scene of the wreck on Sunday, March 13.

The speeding freighter had stranded at near high tide and could not be refloated. Over the years, three salvage companies worked the wreck. The superstructure and the hull down to the waterline were removed. Most of the stern, although broken and scattered, is still there because it was in deeper water and could not easily be dismantled and removed.

The *Wandby* is a beach dive. The wreck site is directly in front of the public parking lot on Ocean Avenue. After entering the water, the diver sees pieces of wreckage and metal plates wedged in crevices in the granite rock. Farther out, in 12 to 14 feet of water, there are large steel plates with I beams attached. As depth increases, the pieces of wreckage are larger. The ship's boiler is about 35 feet deep.

Visibility averages about 15 feet. This wreck is not a good artifact dive, but if the sea is calm and there is no surge, it is a dive for the novice diver. However, most of the wreckage is about 300 feet offshore and if the tide is ebbing, the swim back to shore can be tiring. When planning a dive, the weather, tides, and currents should be carefully considered. Also, divers should tow a buoyed dive flag.

A piece of hull section. Photo by Gary Carbonneau.

Large pieces of the *Wandby* are scattered over the bottom. A diver inspects an I beam. Photo by Gary Carbonneau.

## 28. Unlit Buoy Fatal to Freighter—*Sagamore*

| | | |
|---|---|---|
| **Type of vessel** | : | freighter |
| **Gross tons** | : | 2,592 |
| **Length** | : | 251 feet |
| **Beam** | : | 43.5 feet |
| **Hull construction** | : | steel |
| **Location** | : | 150 yards off Prout's Neck, SW of Cape Elizabeth |
| **Lat. and long.** | : | 43–31.69 N, 70–18.48 W |
| **Approximate depth of water:** | | 20–50 feet |

In a blinding blizzard the Eastern Steamship Line freighter *Sagamore* headed out of Portland, Maine with a general cargo, bound for New York. It was midnight on January 14, 1934.

The ship's captain had received promises of improving weather. One hour and 15 minutes later, however, with heavy snow still falling and the wind close to gale force, the *Sagamore* struck Corwin's Rock.

The freighter's lookouts had been aware of the approaching danger, but as they anxiously stared into the night, with snow lashing their faces,

The *Sagamore* came ashore off the tip of Prout's Neck. Photo from the Ballard Collection by Ralph Blood.

they could not spot the Willard Rock light buoy. That light, marking a dangerous ledge of submerged rocks, was out.

When the *Sagamore* struck, a jagged edge of the rock knifed through her hull as though it were paper instead of steel. Water poured into the holds, and the vessel settled rapidly on Corwin's Rock. The crew of 27 later said they believed the freighter would have gone down with all hands had not a tremendous wave lifted it off the ledge soon after she struck.

The *Sagamore*'s captain realized his ship was sinking and headed to shore, four miles away. The steering apparatus was damaged by the freighter's impact with the rock, severely limiting the ship's maneuverability. After more than an hour, while the terrified crew expected the freighter to founder, the *Sagamore*'s hull grated on the bottom. She was only 150 yards off the tip of Prout's Neck, southwest of Cape Elizabeth.

The blizzard had reduced visibility to zero, and the ship's crew were not aware they were so close to shore. The freighter's decks were awash, driving the crew onto the bridge where they huddled together. The *Sagamore* had grounded at low tide, and all through the night the men watched while huge waves broke over the vessel and the changing tide brought the boiling seas closer to their precarious refuge.

Flares were fired during the night to summon aid. However, the signals went unnoticed, and it was well after dawn before the Coast Guard learned of the *Sagamore*'s plight. It was high tide then and only the freighter's bridge, masts, and funnel projected above water. A resident of Prout's Neck saw the stricken ship and telephoned the Coast Guard station at Cape Elizabeth, whose personnel dispatched a Coast Guard surf-boat to rescue the 27 unharmed men shortly before noon.

The *Sagamore* was a total loss, but a salvage operation lasting eight months removed the cargo and stripped her to the waterline. The freighter's reciprocating steam engine is standing upright, alongside a large generator. A large boiler, steel plates, and other wreckage are scattered over the bottom in 20 to 50 feet of water. The ship's rudder is at a depth of 45 feet. The rocks are covered with kelp and other marine organisms. After severe storms, pieces of steel wreckage wash ashore.

This is an excellent dive for a novice when there is no surge. It is not a beach dive. The land on Prout's Neck is all privately owned, so the wreck site must be approached by boat.

A deck hatch and portholes photographed by Paul Goudreau.

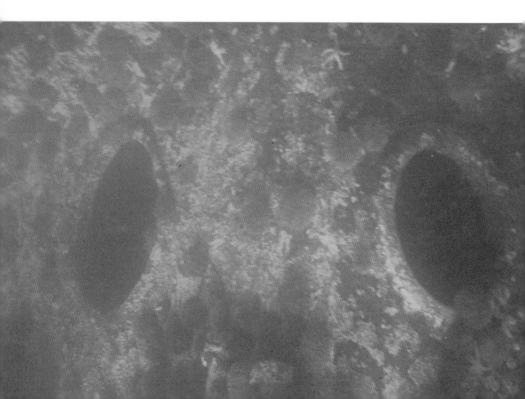

# 29. Huge Sea Rips Off Bow—*Oakey L. Alexander*

| | | |
|---|---|---|
| **Type of vessel** | : | collier |
| **Gross tons** | : | 5,284 |
| **Length** | : | 368.6 feet |
| **Beam** | : | 55.2 feet |
| **Hull construction** | : | steel |
| **Location** | : | Cape Elizabeth |
| **Lat. and long.** | : | 43–33.47 N, 70–12.59 W |
| **Approximate depth of water:** | | 10–40 feet |

Over the weekend of March 1 and 2, 1947, New England was savaged by a northeaster. Barometric pressure lower than that of the area's worst hurricane in 1938 was reported. The pressure dropped to 28.69 compared to 28.91 during the hurricane.

Gale-force winds of 63 miles an hour swept in heavy seas and the huge, pounding waves tossed large boulders onto the coast highway in areas of New Hampshire and Maine. Snow plows were used to push the rubble from the roads, which were impassable in many places.

Lighthouses along the coast received their worst pounding in years as the gale swept seas 50 and 60 feet into the air. At high tide, waves were breaking over Whaleback Lighthouse at Portsmouth.

The collier *Oakey L. Alexander* was built in 1915 for the Pocohontas Steamship Company. The 32-year-old ship, bound for Portland, Maine, with 8,200 tons of coals, was battling the gale and the high seas one mile offshore. Early in the morning of March 3, the third day of the storm, giant seas ripped 150 feet off her bow. Fortunately, the superstructure and stern, containing the 32-man crew, were not damaged. With a show of remarkable seamanship, Captain Raymond Lewis managed to beach the severely crippled collier on the rocky shoals of Cape Elizabeth, Maine, 150 yards offshore. Six other vessels were sunk or stranded by the same storm, which also washed to sea or damaged dozens of summer cottages.

The Coast Guard responded to distress signals from the stranded *Alexander* and rigged up a breeches buoy. A small cannon on shore will fire a line over the rigging of a ship. The line is secured both to the shore and to a high spot on the grounded vessel. A canvas chair-like seat is pulled along the attached line to the ship. A crewman then rides to safety on the breeches buoy, which is being pulled from shore.

For the *Alexander*'s crew, however, riding the breeches buoy was a harrowing experience. The collier lay 150 yards offshore and the heavy crewmen caused the line to sag, and were carried over and through the booming surf to the rocky shore.

Cheers broke from hundreds of spectators as Coast Guardsmen and volunteers hauled the drenched, exhausted men through the breakers. Captain Lewis was last to leave the ship.

The *Oakey L. Alexander*, minus 150 feet of her bow, grounded on the rocky shoals of Cape Elizabeth. Photo courtesy of the U.S. Coast Guard.

The breeches buoy ride was a harrowing experience for the *Oakey Alexander*'s crew. Photo by Gardner Roberts, Portland Press Herald, Portland, Maine.

Another severe storm followed, pushing the *Alexander* 80 feet nearer the shore in about 20 feet of water. A salvage crew recovered about a thousand tons of coal, the superstructure, and part of the hull. The collier's hull, however, is still relatively intact below the waterline. The wreck has collapsed on the port side. The highest areas are 8 to 10 feet. A diver can distinguish and explore several of the ship's compartments. The shaft bed and associated piping can be seen in the engine room. Although the wreck was commercially salvaged, many artifacts can still be recovered, especially after storms.

The wreck is always talking—moaning and groaning. The surge moves metal plates, producing sounds that can be bewildering to a diver.

The depth varies from 10 to 40 feet, and although the wreck is close to shore, it is not a beach dive. The adjacent land is privately owned. There is a boat ramp nearby, but it is in bad condition. Most divers with their own boats launch in Portland, Maine ten miles away. At low tide, some wreckage is exposed, making it easier to find the wreck site.

Visibility is usually good, and the wreck is excellent for novice divers. Be cautious in a surge, however; the ocean can push a diver onto jagged metal or impale him on steel bars that have rusted to a sharp point.

Jim Dolph looking through wreckage. Photo by Gary Carbonneau.

Although the wreck was commercially salvaged and later broken up by storms, there are several compartments divers can explore. Photo by Gary Carbonneau.

# 30. The Lovely Lady—*Lady of the Lake*

| | |
|---|---|
| **Type of vessel** | : passenger liner |
| **Gross tons** | : 120 |
| **Length** | : 125 feet |
| **Beam** | : 35 feet |
| **Hull construction** | : wood |
| **Location** | : Glendale Cove, Lake Winnipesaukee, NH |
| **Approximate depth of water:** | 28 feet |

Lake Winnipesaukee is the largest body of freshwater in New England, considering lakes entirely within the borders of one state. The lake, 25 miles long and 13 miles wide, is centrally located in the state of New Hampshire.

The lake's navigation history begins with the Indians who inhabited the shores and gave it its name. Indian bark canoes were followed, in the early-to mid-1700's, by flat-bottomed sailing vessels called "gundalows."

Next, followed an ingenious idea—the "horseboat." This was a 70-foot boat with a mechanism similar to a treadmill, located near the stern, with two horses walking the treads. This "horsepower" turned two side-wheels.

The steamboat era struck the country in the 1830's, and Lake Winnipesaukee was not to be left behind. The first Winnipesaukee steamboat to exceed 100 feet in length was the side-wheeler *Lady of the Lake*. She was built in 1848–49 by the Winnipesaukee Steamboat Company to carry passengers and freight.

Hundreds gathered from around the state to witness her launching and to marvel at her size, considered tremendous for that period. Many expected the new side-wheeler to capsize as she slid down the ways. However, when the shores were knocked away from the hull, she slid gracefully into the water.

The steamer, with a capacity for 400 passengers, was later sold to the Concord and Montreal Railroad. The *Lady*, as she was known, was the most popular steamer on the lake, holding sway over commercial navigation until the *Mount Washington* was launched in 1872. That steamer, 50 feet longer than the *Lady*, was the largest and would become the most famous in Winnipesaukee's history. The *Lady* and the *Mount* were rivals for 21 years, with the newer side-wheeler slowly, but steadily, displacing the aging steamer.

On September 19, 1893, in Lakeport where she had been built almost a half-century before, the *Lady*'s superstructure was dismantled and her machinery removed. The decks and cabins, however, were intact, so the following year the gutted steamer was towed to Glendale and used as a boarding house for workmen building what is now called Kimball's Castle. Benjamin Kimball, owner of the Concord and Montreal Railroad and the

The side-wheeler *Lady of the Lake* early in her 44-year career. Photo courtesy of Jim Dolph.

A diver inspects a deck support. Note the white paint. Photo by Gary Carbonneau.

*Lady*, developed an infatuation with castles during a trip to Europe. On returning, he had a castle-like home built on Lake Winnipesaukee.

In 1895, it was decided to sink the *Lady* in deep water off Rattlesnake Island. Her hull was filled with rocks, but while under tow she foundered and sank in 28 feet of water in the middle of Glendale Cove. The *Lady*'s beautiful gold and white figurehead, a lady with a paddle in hand, had been removed before her sinking and can be seen today at the old Historical Building on North Main Street in Concord.

The *Lady*, sitting upright, rises about 12 feet off the bottom. The hull and first deck are almost intact and the wreck is easy to penetrate. Paint can still be seen on some planking. The *Lady* is excellent for novice divers, except for the location—just outside a marina with heavy boat traffic during the summer months. Divers should come up the anchor line and use a dive flag. Because of the boat traffic and aquatic organisms, visibility averages only about 20 feet in the summer. The wreck site is usually marked with a plastic jug or some other float.

The *Lady* is also used for ice dives. Dive clubs and other groups usually keep the hole in the ice open all winter. At that time of year, with a decrease in aquatic growth and no waves or boat traffic stirring up the sediment, visibility is at its best. A safetly line should be used on any ice dive.

The wreck site is about 200 yards from shore, but there is no launching ramp in the immediate area. Launching, rentals and charters are available about a half-hour boat ride away in Wolfeboro.

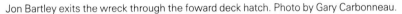

Jon Bartley exits the wreck through the foward deck hatch. Photo by Gary Carbonneau.

Jim Dolph looking through a
starboard port. The photo
was taken from the interior
by Gary Carbonneau.

Fantail ribs can be seen above the scuttling stones in the *Lady*'s stern. Photo by Gary Carbonneau.

# APPENDIX A: Dive Charter Boats

| Boat or Company | Contact | Telephone | Dockage |
|---|---|---|---|
| Wahoo | Steve Bielenda | (516) 928-3849 | Captree State Park, L.I., N.Y. |
| Baccala | Jack Fiora | (203) 873-8488 | Mystic, CT |
| Scuba Shack | Scuba Shack | (203) 563-0119 | Stonington, CT |
| Sea Turtle | Scuba Shack | (203) 563-0119 | New London, CT |
| Pilot Fish III | Bill Palmer | (203) 269-0619 | Snug Harbor, Pt. Judith, RI |
| Argonaut | Frank Long | (401) 789-7672 | Snug Harbor, Pt. Judith, RI |
| Miss Corky R | Frank Benoit | (617) 339-5995 | Westport, MA |
| Open Water Charters | Rich Fratto | (617) 848-4990 | Danversport, MA |
| Cape Cod Divers Inc. | B.G. Sykes | (800) 348-4641 | Harwichport, MA |
| Andy-Lynns | Mario Costa | (617) 746-4922 | Plymouth, MA |
| Anaconda | Mark Condon | (617) 834-7904 | Plymouth, MA |
| Three Js | Perry Luke | (617) 327-3360 | Beverly, MA |
| North Country Scuba | North Country Scuba | (603) 569-2120 | Wolfeboro (Lake Win.), NH |
| Saco Bay Diving & Charters | Paul Goudreau | (207) 934-2870 | Old Orchard Beach, ME |
| The Dive Boat | Tommy's Dive Shop | (207) 797-8563 | Portland, ME |
| Custom Outfitters & Expeditions | Robert Bernstein | (207) 372-8220 | Tenants Harbor, ME |